MznLnx

Missing Links Exam Preps

Exam Prep for

Management

Hitt, Black & Porter, 2nd Edition

The MznLnx Exam Prep is your link from the texbook and lecture to your exams.
The MznLnx Exam Preps are unauthorized and comprehensive reviews of your textbooks.

All material provided by MznLnx and Rico Publications (c) 2010
Textbook publishers and textbook authors do not particpate in or contribute to these reviews.

MznLnx

Rico Publications

Exam Prep for Management
2nd Edition
Hitt, Black & Porter

Publisher: Raymond Houge
Assistant Editor: Michael Rouger
Text and Cover Designer: Lisa Buckner
Marketing Manager: Sara Swagger
Project Manager, Editorial Production: Jerry Emerson
Art Director: Vernon Lowerui

Product Manager: Dave Mason
Editorial Assitant: Rachel Guzmanji
Pedagogy: Debra Long
Cover Image: Jim Reed/Getty Images
Text and Cover Printer: City Printing, Inc.
Compositor: Media Mix, Inc.

(c) 2010 Rico Publications
ALL RIGHTS RESERVED. No part of this work covered by the copyright may be reproduced or used in any form or by an means--graphic, electronic, or mechanical, including photocopying, recording, taping, Web distribution, information storage, and retrieval systems, or in any other manner--without the written permission of the publisher.

Printed in the United States
ISBN:

For more information about our products, contact us at:
Dave.Mason@RicoPublications.com

For permission to use material from this text or product, submit a request online to:
Dave.Mason@RicoPublications.com

Contents

CHAPTER 1
The Nature of Management   1

CHAPTER 2
Social Responsibility and Managerial Ethics   7

CHAPTER 3
International Management and Globalization   10

CHAPTER 4
Individual and Group Decision Making   15

CHAPTER 5
Strategic Management   19

CHAPTER 6
Planning   27

CHAPTER 7
Organizational Structure and Design   31

CHAPTER 8
Managing Diverse Human Resources   35

CHAPTER 9
Leadership   50

CHAPTER 10
Motivation   54

CHAPTER 11
Groups and Teams   58

CHAPTER 12
Communication and Negotiation   62

CHAPTER 13
Operations Management   64

CHAPTER 14
Control   74

CHAPTER 15
Organizational Change and Development   78

ANSWER KEY   85

TO THE STUDENT

COMPREHENSIVE

The *MznLnx* Exam Prep series is designed to help you pass your exams. Editors at MznLnx review your textbooks and then prepare these practice exams to help you master the textbook material. Unlike study guides, workbooks, and practice tests provided by the texbook publisher and textbook authors, *MznLnx* gives you **all** of the material in each chapter in exam form, not just samples, so you can be sure to nail your exam.

MECHANICAL

The MznLnx Exam Prep series creates exams that will help you learn the subject matter as well as test you on your understanding. Each question is designed to help you master the concept. Just working through the exams, you gain an understanding of the subject--its a simple mechanical process that produces success.

INTEGRATED STUDY GUIDE AND REVIEW

MznLnx is not just a set of exams designed to test you, its also a comprehensive review of the subject content. Each exam question is also a review of the concept, making sure that you will get the answer correct without having to go to other sources of material. You learn as you go! Its the easiest way to pass an exam.

HUMOR

Studying can be tedious and dry. MznLnx's instructional design includes moderate humor within the exam questions on occassion, to break the tedium and revitalize the brain

Chapter 1. The Nature of Management

1. _____ is a type of trade policy that allows traders to act and transact without interference from government. Thus, the policy permits trading partners mutual gains from trade, with goods and services produced according to the theory of comparative advantage.

   Under a _____ policy, prices are a reflection of true supply and demand, and are the sole determinant of resource allocation.

   a. Free Trade
   b. 1990 Clean Air Act
   c. 33 Strategies of War
   d. 28-hour day

2. _____ is a designated group of countries that have agreed to eliminate tariffs, quotas and preferences on most (if not all) goods and services traded between them. It can be considered the second stage of economic integration. Countries choose this kind of economic integration form if their economical structures are complementary.

   a. 1990 Clean Air Act
   b. 33 Strategies of War
   c. 28-hour day
   d. Free trade area

3. The _____ was the outcome of the failure of negotiating governments to create the International Trade Organization (ITO.) GATT was formed in 1947 and lasted until 1994, when it was replaced by the World Trade Organization. The Bretton Woods Conference had introduced the idea for an organization to regulate trade as part of a larger plan for economic recovery after World War II.

   a. Multilateral treaty
   b. 1990 Clean Air Act
   c. 28-hour day
   d. General Agreement on Tariffs and Trade

4. _____ in its literal sense is the process of transformation of local or regional phenomena into global ones. It can be described as a process by which the people of the world are unified into a single society and function together.

   This process is a combination of economic, technological, sociocultural and political forces.

   a. Collaborative Planning, Forecasting and Replenishment
   b. Histogram
   c. Cost Management
   d. Globalization

Chapter 1. The Nature of Management

5. The _____ is a trilateral trade bloc in North America created by the governments of the United States, Canada, and Mexico. The agreement creating the trade bloc came into force on January 1, 1994. It superseded the Canada-United States Free Trade Agreement between the U.S. and Canada.
   a. Trade union
   b. Business war game
   c. Career portfolios
   d. North American Free Trade Agreement

6. Procter is a surname, and may also refer to:

   - Bryan Waller Procter (pseud. Barry Cornwall), English poet
   - Goodwin Procter, American law firm
   - _____, consumer products multinational

   a. Strict liability
   b. Master and Servant Acts
   c. Downstream
   d. Procter ' Gamble

7. _____ according to Onuoha (2007) is the practice of starting new organizations or revitalizing mature organizations, particularly new businesses generally in response to identified opportunities. _____ is often a difficult undertaking, as a vast majority of new businesses fail. Entrepreneurial activities are substantially different depending on the type of organization that is being started.
   a. AAAI
   b. A4e
   c. Entrepreneurship
   d. A Stake in the Outcome

8. _____ is one of the managerial functions like planning, organizing, staffing and directing. It is an important function because it helps to check the errors and to take the corrective action so that deviation from standards are minimized and stated goals of the organization are achieved in desired manner. According to modern concepts, _____ is a foreseeing action whereas earlier concept of _____ was used only when errors were detected. _____ in management means setting standards, measuring actual performance and taking corrective action.
   a. Decision tree pruning
   b. Turnover
   c. Schedule of reinforcement
   d. Control

Chapter 1. The Nature of Management

9. Maslow's _____ is a theory in psychology, proposed by Abraham Maslow in his 1943 paper A Theory of Human Motivation, which he subsequently extended to include his observations of humans' innate curiosity.

Maslow's _____ is predetermined in order of importance. It is often depicted as a pyramid consisting of five levels: the lowest level is associated with physiological needs, while the uppermost level is associated with self-actualization needs, particularly those related to identity and purpose. Deficiency needs must be met first. Once these are met, seeking to satisfy growth needs drives personal growth. The higher needs in this hierarchy only come into focus when the lower needs in the pyramid are met.

   a. Hierarchy of needs
   b. 28-hour day
   c. 33 Strategies of War
   d. 1990 Clean Air Act

10. _____ are job factors that can cause dissatisfaction if missing but do not necessarily motivate employees if increased.

_____ have mostly to do with the job environment. These factors are important or notable only when they are lacking.

   a. Work system
   b. Hygiene factors
   c. Split shift
   d. Work-at-home scheme

11. The _____ was a period in the late 18th and early 19th centuries when major changes in agriculture, manufacturing, mining, and transportation had a profound effect on the socioeconomic and cultural conditions in Britain. The changes subsequently spread throughout Europe, North America, and eventually the world. The onset of the _____ marked a major turning point in human society; almost every aspect of daily life was eventually influenced in some way.
   a. Affiliation
   b. Adam Smith
   c. Abraham Harold Maslow
   d. Industrial Revolution

12. _____ is an attempt to motivate employees by giving them the opportunity to use the range of their abilities. It is an idea that was developed by the American psychologist Frederick Herzberg in the 1950s. It can be contrasted to job enlargement which simply increases the number of tasks without changing the challenge.

a. Cash cow
b. Catfish effect
c. C-A-K-E
d. Job enrichment

13. _____ is a theory of management that analyzes and synthesizes workflows, with the objective of improving labour productivity. The core ideas of the theory were developed by Frederick Winslow Taylor in the 1880s and 1890s, and were first published in his monographs, Shop Management and The Principles of _____ Taylor believed that decisions based upon tradition and rules of thumb should be replaced by precise procedures developed after careful study of an individual at work.

a. Master production schedule
b. Capacity planning
c. Value engineering
d. Scientific management

14. Theory X and _____ are theories of human motivation created and developed by Douglas McGregor at the MIT Sloan School of Management in the 1960s that have been used in human resource management, organizational behavior, organizational communication and organizational development. They describe two very different attitudes toward workforce motivation. McGregor felt that companies followed either one or the other approach.

In _____, management assumes employees may be ambitious and self-motivated and exercise self-control. It is believed that employees enjoy their mental and physical work duties.

a. Theory Y
b. Contingency theory
c. Business Workflow Analysis
d. Design leadership

15. A _____ is a business efficiency technique combining the Time Study work of Frederick Winslow Taylor with the Motion Study work of Frank and Lillian Gilbreth (not to be confused with their son, best known through the biographical 1950 film and book Cheaper by the Dozen.) It is a major part of scientific management (Taylorism.)

A _____ would be used to reduce the number of motions in performing a task in order to increase productivity.

a. Total benefits of ownership
b. Manufacturing operations
c. Prevailing wage
d. Time and motion study

16. A _____ is a list of the general tasks and responsibilities of a position. Typically, it also includes to whom the position reports, specifications such as the qualifications needed by the person in the job, salary range for the position, etc. A _____ is usually developed by conducting a job analysis, which includes examining the tasks and sequences of tasks necessary to perform the job.
   a. Recruitment
   b. Job description
   c. Recruitment Process Insourcing
   d. Recruitment advertising

17. In politics, a _____, (by metaphor with the carved _____ at the prow of a sailing ship), is a person who holds an important title or office yet executes little actual power, most commonly limited by convention rather than law. Common _____s include constitutional monarchs, such as: Queen Elizabeth II, the Emperor of Japan, or presidents in parliamentary democracies, such as the President of Israel.

While the authority of a _____ is in practice generally symbolic, public opinion, respect for the office or the office holder and access to high levels of government can give them significant influence on events.

   a. 28-hour day
   b. 33 Strategies of War
   c. 1990 Clean Air Act
   d. Figurehead

18. In economics, _____ is the desire to own something and the ability to pay for it. The term _____ signifies the ability or the willingness to buy a particular commodity at a given point of time.
   a. Demand
   b. 28-hour day
   c. 33 Strategies of War
   d. 1990 Clean Air Act

19. _____ consists of the mental process of thinking involved with the process of judging the merits of multiple options and selecting one of them for action. Some simple examples include deciding whether to get up in the morning or go back to sleep, or selecting a given route for a journey. More complex examples (often decisions that affect what a person thinks or their core beliefs) include choosing a lifestyle, religious affiliation, or political position.

a. Championship mobilization
b. Trade study
c. Groups decision making
d. Choice

20. '_____' refers to mental and communicative algorithms applied during social communications and interactions in order to reach certain effects or results. The term '_____' is used often in business contexts to refer to the measure of a person's ability to operate within business organizations through social communication and interactions. _____ are how people relate to one another.
a. A Stake in the Outcome
b. A4e
c. AAAI
d. Interpersonal skills

Chapter 2. Social Responsibility and Managerial Ethics

1. Many negative _____ are related to the environmental consequences of production and use

   - Systemic risk describes the risks to the overall economy arising from the risks which the banking system takes. That the private costs of banking failure may be smaller than the social costs justifies banking regulations, although regulations could create a moral hazard.

   - Anthropogenic climate change is attributed to greenhouse gas emissions from burning oil, gas, and coal. Global warming has been ranked as the #1 externality of all economic activity, in the magnitude of potential harms and yet remains unmitigated.

   a. AAAI
   b. A Stake in the Outcome
   c. A4e
   d. Externalities

2. _____ is a concept whereby a person's financial liability is limited to a fixed sum, most commonly the value of a person's investment in a company or partnership with _____. In other words, if a company with _____ is sued, then the plaintiffs are suing the company, not its owners or investors. A shareholder in a limited company is not personally liable for any of the debts of the company, other than for the value of his investment in that company.
   a. Toxic Substances Control Act
   b. Partnership
   c. Limited liability
   d. Privity

3. _____ is a form of corporate self-regulation integrated into a business model. Ideally, _____ policy would function as a built-in, self-regulating mechanism whereby business would monitor and ensure their adherence to law, ethical standards, and international norms. Business would embrace responsibility for the impact of their activities on the environment, consumers, employees, communities, stakeholders and all other members of the public sphere.
   a. 33 Strategies of War
   b. Corporate Social responsibility
   c. 1990 Clean Air Act
   d. 28-hour day

4. A _____ is a relatively new executive level position at a corporation, company, organization typically reporting directly to the CEO or board of directors. The _____ is responsible for a brand's image, experience, and promise, and propagating it throughout all aspects of the company. The brand officer oversees marketing, advertising, design, public relations and customer service departments.

a. Chief brand officer
b. Purchasing manager
c. Director of communications
d. Chief executive officer

5. An _____ is a situation that will often involve an apparent conflict between moral imperatives, in which to obey one would result in transgressing another. This is also called an ethical paradox since in moral philosophy, paradox plays a central role in ethics debates. For instance, an ethical admonition to 'love thy neighbour as thy self' is not always just in contrast with, but sometimes in contradiction to an armed neighbour actively trying to kill you: if he or she succeeds, you will not be able to love him or her.
a. Ethical dilemma
b. AAAI
c. A Stake in the Outcome
d. A4e

6. _____ can be regarded as an outcome of mental processes (cognitive process) leading to the selection of a course of action among several alternatives. Every _____ process produces a final choice. The output can be an action or an opinion of choice.
a. 1990 Clean Air Act
b. 28-hour day
c. 33 Strategies of War
d. Decision making

7. In US employment law, _____ is defined as a substantially different rate of selection in hiring, promotion sex statistical significance tests, and/or practical significance tests. _____ is often used interchangeably with 'disparate impact,' which was a legal term coined in one of the most significant U.S. Supreme Court rulings on disparate or _____: Griggs v. Duke Power Co., 1971.
a. Adverse impact
b. A Stake in the Outcome
c. AAAI
d. A4e

8. _____ is a way of expressing knowledge or belief that an event will occur or has occurred. In mathematics the concept has been given an exact meaning in _____ theory, that is used extensively in such areas of study as mathematics, statistics, finance, gambling, science, and philosophy to draw conclusions about the likelihood of potential events and the underlying mechanics of complex systems.

The word _____ does not have a consistent direct definition.

a. Statistics
b. Standard deviation
c. Time series analysis
d. Probability

9. The _____ of 1977 (15 U.S.C. §§ 78dd-1, et seq.) is a United States federal law known primarily for two of its main provisions, one that addresses accounting transparency requirements under the Securities Exchange Act of 1934 and another concerning bribery of foreign officials.
   a. Limited liability
   b. Meritor Savings Bank v. Vinson
   c. Social Security Act of 1965
   d. Foreign Corrupt Practices Act

Chapter 3. International Management and Globalization

1. _____ in its literal sense is the process of transformation of local or regional phenomena into global ones. It can be described as a process by which the people of the world are unified into a single society and function together.

This process is a combination of economic, technological, sociocultural and political forces.

   a. Globalization
   b. Histogram
   c. Collaborative Planning, Forecasting and Replenishment
   d. Cost Management

2. The _____ of 2002 (Pub.L. 107-204, 116 Stat. 745, enacted July 30, 2002), also known as the Public Company Accounting Reform and Investor Protection Act of 2002 and commonly called Sarbanes-Oxley, Sarbox or SOX, is a United States federal law enacted on July 30, 2002, as a reaction to a number of major corporate and accounting scandals including those affecting Enron, Tyco International, Adelphia, Peregrine Systems and WorldCom.
   a. Letter of credit
   b. Sarbanes-Oxley Act
   c. Fair Labor Standards Act
   d. Sarbanes-Oxley Act of 2002

3. _____ refers to the movement of cash into or out of a business or financial product. It is usually measured during a specified, finite period of time. Measurement of _____ can be used

   - to determine a project's rate of return or value. The time of _____s into and out of projects are used as inputs in financial models such as internal rate of return, and net present value.
   - to determine problems with a business's liquidity. Being profitable does not necessarily mean being liquid. A company can fail because of a shortage of cash, even while profitable.
   - as an alternate measure of a business's profits when it is believed that accrual accounting concepts do not represent economic realities. For example, a company may be notionally profitable but generating little operational cash (as may be the case for a company that barters its products rather than selling for cash.) In such a case, the company may be deriving additional operating cash by issuing shares evaluating default risk, re-investment requirements, etc.

   _____ is a generic term used differently depending on the context. It may be defined by users for their own purposes.

   a. Cash flow
   b. Gross profit
   c. Sweat equity
   d. Gross profit margin

Chapter 3. International Management and Globalization

4. _____ is a term used to describe any moral, political that stresses human interdependence and the importance of a collective, rather than the importance of separate individuals. Collectivists focus on community and society, and seek to give priority to group goals over individual goals. The philosophical underpinnings of _____ are for some related to holism or organicism - the view that the whole is greater than the sum of its parts/pieces.
    a. Collaborative methods
    b. 28-hour day
    c. 1990 Clean Air Act
    d. Collectivism

5. _____ is exchange of capital, goods, and services across international borders or territories. In most countries, it represents a significant share of gross domestic product (GDP.) While _____ has been present throughout much of history, its economic, social, and political importance has been on the rise in recent centuries.
    a. A Stake in the Outcome
    b. A4e
    c. AAAI
    d. International trade

6. A _____ is a formal relationship between two or more parties to pursue a set of agreed upon goals or to meet a critical business need while remaining independent organizations.

    Partners may provide the _____ with resources such as products, distribution channels, manufacturing capability, project funding, capital equipment, knowledge, expertise, or intellectual property. The alliance is a cooperation or collaboration which aims for a synergy where each partner hopes that the benefits from the alliance will be greater than those from individual efforts.

    a. Golden parachute
    b. Process automation
    c. Strategic alliance
    d. Farmshoring

7. _____ describes the relocation by a company of a business process from one country to another -- typically an operational process, such as manufacturing such as accounting. Even state governments employ _____.

    The term is in use in several distinct but closely related ways.

a. A Stake in the Outcome
b. AAAI
c. A4e
d. Offshoring

8. _____ is subcontracting a process, such as product design or manufacturing, to a third-party company. The decision to outsource is often made in the interest of lowering cost or making better use of time and energy costs, redirecting or conserving energy directed at the competencies of a particular business, or to make more efficient use of land, labor, capital, (information) technology and resources. _____ became part of the business lexicon during the 1980s.

   a. Outsourcing
   b. Opinion leadership
   c. Operant conditioning
   d. Unemployment insurance

9. _____ is an advertisement in which a particular product specifically mentions a competitor by name for the express purpose of showing why the competitor is inferior to the product naming it.

This should not be confused with parody advertisements, where a fictional product is being advertised for the purpose of poking fun at the particular advertisement, nor should it be confused with the use of a coined brand name for the purpose of comparing the product without actually naming an actual competitor. ('Wikipedia tastes better and is less filling than the Encyclopedia Galactica.')

In the 1980s, during what has been referred to as the cola wars, soft-drink manufacturer Pepsi ran a series of advertisements where people, caught on hidden camera, in a blind taste test, chose Pepsi over rival Coca-Cola.

   a. 33 Strategies of War
   b. Comparative advertising
   c. 1990 Clean Air Act
   d. 28-hour day

10. The phrase mergers and _____s refers to the aspect of corporate strategy, corporate finance and management dealing with the buying, selling and combining of different companies that can aid, finance, or help a growing company in a given industry grow rapidly without having to create another business entity.

An _____, also known as a takeover or a buyout, is the buying of one company (the 'target') by another. An _____ may be friendly or hostile.

a. A Stake in the Outcome
b. A4e
c. AAAI
d. Acquisition

11. A _____, in business matters, is an entity that is controlled by a bigger and more powerful entity. The controlled entity is called a company, corporation, or limited liability company and in some cases can be a government or state-owned enterprise, and the controlling entity is called its parent (or the parent company.) The reason for this distinction is that a lone company cannot be a _____ of any organization; only an entity representing a legal fiction as a separate entity can be a _____.

a. 28-hour day
b. Subsidiary
c. 33 Strategies of War
d. 1990 Clean Air Act

12. An _____ is a person who has possession of an enterprise and assumes significant accountability for the inherent risks and the outcome. It is an ambitious leader who combines land, labor, and capital to create and market new goods or services. The term is a loanword from French and was first defined by the Irish economist Richard Cantillon.

a. A4e
b. AAAI
c. A Stake in the Outcome
d. Entrepreneur

13. _____ is one of the managerial functions like planning, organizing, staffing and directing. It is an important function because it helps to check the errors and to take the corrective action so that deviation from standards are minimized and stated goals of the organization are achieved in desired manner. According to modern concepts, _____ is a foreseeing action whereas earlier concept of _____ was used only when errors were detected. _____ in management means setting standards, measuring actual performance and taking corrective action.

a. Turnover
b. Schedule of reinforcement
c. Decision tree pruning
d. Control

14. A _____ is a process in which a potential employee is evaluated by an employer for prospective employment in their company, organization and was established in the late 16th century.

Chapter 3. International Management and Globalization

A _____ typically precedes the hiring decision, and is used to evaluate the candidate. The interview is usually preceded by the evaluation of submitted résumés from interested candidates, then selecting a small number of candidates for interviews.

a. Supported employment
b. Split shift
c. Payrolling
d. Job interview

15. A _____ -- also known as a geographically dispersed team -- is a group of individuals who work across time, space, and organizational boundaries with links strengthened by webs of communication technology. They have complementary skills and are committed to a common purpose, have interdependent performance goals, and share an approach to work for which they hold themselves mutually accountable. Geographically dispersed teams allow organizations to hire and retain the best people regardless of location.

a. Risk management
b. Kanban
c. Virtual team
d. Trademark

16. Procter is a surname, and may also refer to:

- Bryan Waller Procter (pseud. Barry Cornwall), English poet
- Goodwin Procter, American law firm
- _____, consumer products multinational

a. Downstream
b. Strict liability
c. Master and Servant Acts
d. Procter ' Gamble

Chapter 4. Individual and Group Decision Making

1. _____ can be regarded as an outcome of mental processes (cognitive process) leading to the selection of a course of action among several alternatives. Every _____ process produces a final choice. The output can be an action or an opinion of choice.
   a. 1990 Clean Air Act
   b. Decision making
   c. 33 Strategies of War
   d. 28-hour day

2. _____ is an advertisement in which a particular product specifically mentions a competitor by name for the express purpose of showing why the competitor is inferior to the product naming it.

   This should not be confused with parody advertisements, where a fictional product is being advertised for the purpose of poking fun at the particular advertisement, nor should it be confused with the use of a coined brand name for the purpose of comparing the product without actually naming an actual competitor. ('Wikipedia tastes better and is less filling than the Encyclopedia Galactica.')

   In the 1980s, during what has been referred to as the cola wars, soft-drink manufacturer Pepsi ran a series of advertisements where people, caught on hidden camera, in a blind taste test, chose Pepsi over rival Coca-Cola.

   a. 28-hour day
   b. 1990 Clean Air Act
   c. 33 Strategies of War
   d. Comparative advertising

3. In economics, _____ is a measure of the relative satisfaction from consumption of various goods and services. Given this measure, one may speak meaningfully of increasing or decreasing _____, and thereby explain economic behavior in terms of attempts to increase one's _____. For illustrative purposes, changes in _____ are sometimes expressed in units called utils.
   a. Indirect utility function
   b. Ordinal utility
   c. Utility
   d. A Stake in the Outcome

4. _____ is a concept based on the fact that rationality of individuals is limited by the information they have, the cognitive limitations of their minds, and the finite amount of time they have to make decisions. This contrasts with the concept of rationality as optimization. Another way to look at _____ is that, because decision-makers lack the ability and resources to arrive at the optimal solution, they instead apply their rationality only after having greatly simplified the choices available.

Chapter 4. Individual and Group Decision Making

   a. Transferable utility
   b. Bounded rationality
   c. Mixed strategy
   d. Complete information

5. _____ is an adjective for experience-based techniques that help in problem solving, learning and discovery. A _____ method is particularly used to rapidly come to a solution that is hoped to be close to the best possible answer, or 'optimal solution'. _____s are 'rules of thumb', educated guesses, intuitive judgments or simply common sense.
   a. Representativeness
   b. Heuristic
   c. 28-hour day
   d. 1990 Clean Air Act

6. Appraisal is the third and last stage in using formal decision methods. The objective of the appraisal stage is for the decision maker to develop insight into the decision and determine a clear course of action. Much of the insight developed in this stage results from exploring the implications of the formal _____ developed during the formulation stage (i.e., from mining the model.)
   a. Kepner-Tregoe
   b. Decision model
   c. Nominal group technique
   d. Decision Matrix

7. A _____ is a set of instructions having the force of a directive, covering those features of operations that lend themselves to a definite or standardized procedure without loss of effectiveness. Standard Operating Policies and Procedures can be effective catalysts to drive performance improvement and improving organizational results.
   a. Standard operating procedure
   b. Risk-benefit analysis
   c. 1990 Clean Air Act
   d. Longitudinal study

8. _____ is decision making in groups consisting of multiple members/entities. The challenge of group decision is deciding what action a group should take. There are various systems designed to solve this problem.
   a. Groups decision making
   b. Control of Substances Hazardous to Health Regulations 2002
   c. Collaborative Planning, Forecasting and Replenishment
   d. Genbutsu

9. _____ is a type of thought exhibited by group members who try to minimize conflict and reach consensus without critically testing, analyzing, and evaluating ideas. Individual creativity, uniqueness, and independent thinking are lost in the pursuit of group cohesiveness, as are the advantages of reasonable balance in choice and thought that might normally be obtained by making decisions as a group. During _____, members of the group avoid promoting viewpoints outside the comfort zone of consensus thinking.
   a. Self-report inventory
   b. Diffusion of responsibility
   c. Psychological statistics
   d. Groupthink

10. _____ is complete agreement by everyone. When unanimous, everybody is of same mind and acting together as one. Many groups consider unanimous decisions a sign of agreement, solidarity, and unity.
    a. AAAI
    b. A4e
    c. Unanimity
    d. A Stake in the Outcome

11. A _____ is a group of employees from various functional areas of the organization - research, engineering, marketing, finance. human resources, and operations, for example - who are all focused on a specific objective and are responsible to work as a team to improve coordination and innovation across divisions and resolve mutual problems.
    a. Cross-functional team
    b. Sociotechnical systems
    c. Goal-setting theory
    d. Graduate recruitment

12. A _____ is a process in which a potential employee is evaluated by an employer for prospective employment in their company, organization and was established in the late 16th century.

A _____ typically precedes the hiring decision, and is used to evaluate the candidate. The interview is usually preceded by the evaluation of submitted résumés from interested candidates, then selecting a small number of candidates for interviews.

   a. Supported employment
   b. Payrolling
   c. Split shift
   d. Job interview

Chapter 4. Individual and Group Decision Making

13. _____ is a group creativity technique designed to generate a large number of ideas for the solution of a problem. The method was first popularized in the late 1930s by Alex Faickney Osborn in a book called Applied Imagination. Osborn proposed that groups could double their creative output with _____.
    a. Affiliation
    b. Abraham Harold Maslow
    c. Adam Smith
    d. Brainstorming

14. _____ is the pursuit of influencing outcomes -- including public-policy and resource allocation decisions within political, economic, and social systems and institutions -- that directly affect people's current lives. (Cohen, 2001)

    Therefore, _____ can be seen as a deliberate process of speaking out on issues of concern in order to exert some influence on behalf of ideas or persons. Based on this definition, Cohen (2001) states that 'ideologues of all persuasions advocate' to bring a change in people's lives.

    a. A4e
    b. AAAI
    c. A Stake in the Outcome
    d. Advocacy

15. The _____ is a systematic, interactive forecasting method which relies on a panel of independent experts. The carefully selected experts answer questionnaires in two or more rounds. After each round, a facilitator provides an anonymous summary of the experts' forecasts from the previous round as well as the reasons they provided for their judgments.
    a. Learning organization
    b. Delphi method
    c. Hoshin Kanri
    d. Quality function deployment

16. The _____ is a decision making method for use among groups of many sizes, who want to make their decision quickly, as by a vote, but want everyone's opinions taken into account (as opposed to traditional voting, where only the largest group is considered). The method of tallying is the difference. First, every member of the group gives their view of the solution, with a short explanation.
    a. Decision model
    b. Hierarchical Decision Process
    c. Belief decision matrix
    d. Nominal group technique

Chapter 5. Strategic Management

1. _____ is, in very basic words, a position a firm occupies against its competitors.

According to Michael Porter, the three methods for creating a sustainable _____ are through:

1. Cost leadership

2. Differentiation

3. Focus (economics)

   a. Theory Z
   b. 1990 Clean Air Act
   c. 28-hour day
   d. Competitive advantage

2. In economics, business, retail, and accounting, a _____ is the value of money that has been used up to produce something, and hence is not available for use anymore. In economics, a _____ is an alternative that is given up as a result of a decision. In business, the _____ may be one of acquisition, in which case the amount of money expended to acquire it is counted as _____.
   a. Cost overrun
   b. Fixed costs
   c. Cost allocation
   d. Cost

3. _____ is a concept developed by Michael Porter, used in business strategy. It describes a way to establish the competitive advantage. _____, in basic words, means the lowest cost of operation in the industry.
   a. Cost leadership
   b. Strategic business unit
   c. Strategic group
   d. Switching cost

4. _____ has been described as the 'process of social influence in which one person can enlist the aid and support of others in the accomplishment of a common task' . A definition more inclusive of followers comes from Alan Keith of Genentech who said '_____ is ultimately about creating a way for people to contribute to making something extraordinary happen.'

_____ is one of the most salient aspects of the organizational context. However, defining _____ has been challenging.

a. 1990 Clean Air Act
b. 28-hour day
c. Situational leadership
d. Leadership

5. A _____ is a brief written statement of the purpose of a company or organization. Ideally, a _____ guides the actions of the organization, spells out its overall goal, provides a sense of direction, and guides decision making for all levels of management.

_____s often contain the following:

- Purpose and aim of the organization
- The organization's primary stakeholders: clients, stockholders, etc.
- Responsibilities of the organization toward these stakeholders
- Products and services offered

In developing a _____:

- Encourage as much input as feasible from employees, volunteers, and other stakeholders
- Publicize it broadly

The _____ can be used to resolve differences between business stakeholders. Stakeholders include: employees including managers and executives, stockholders, board of directors, customers, suppliers, distributors, creditors, governments (local, state, federal, etc.), unions, competitors, NGO's, and the general public.

a. 1990 Clean Air Act
b. 33 Strategies of War
c. 28-hour day
d. Mission statement

6. _____ is an organization's process of defining its strategy and making decisions on allocating its resources to pursue this strategy, including its capital and people. Various business analysis techniques can be used in _____, including SWOT analysis (Strengths, Weaknesses, Opportunities, and Threats) and PEST analysis (Political, Economic, Social, and Technological analysis) or STEER analysis involving Socio-cultural, Technological, Economic, Ecological, and Regulatory factors and EPISTEL (Environment, Political, Informatic, Social, Technological, Economic and Legal)

Chapter 5. Strategic Management

_____ is the formal consideration of an organization's future course. All _____ deals with at least one of three key questions:

1. 'What do we do?'
2. 'For whom do we do it?'
3. 'How do we excel?'

In business _____, the third question is better phrased 'How can we beat or avoid competition?'. (Bradford and Duncan, page 1.)

a. 28-hour day
b. 1990 Clean Air Act
c. 33 Strategies of War
d. Strategic planning

7. _____ is a process of planning and controlling the performance or execution of any type of activity, such as:

- a project (project _____) or
- a process (process _____, sometimes referred to as the process performance measurement and management system.)

Organization's senior management is responsible for carrying out its _____.

a. Participatory management
b. Management process
c. Work design
d. Human Relations Movement

8. _____ is one of the managerial functions like planning, organizing, staffing and directing. It is an important function because it helps to check the errors and to take the corrective action so that deviation from standards are minimized and stated goals of the organization are achieved in desired manner. According to modern concepts, _____ is a foreseeing action whereas earlier concept of _____ was used only when errors were detected. _____ in management means setting standards, measuring actual performance and taking corrective action.

a. Turnover
b. Control
c. Decision tree pruning
d. Schedule of reinforcement

Chapter 5. Strategic Management

9. Procter is a surname, and may also refer to:

   - Bryan Waller Procter (pseud. Barry Cornwall), English poet
   - Goodwin Procter, American law firm
   - _____, consumer products multinational

   a. Downstream
   b. Procter ' Gamble
   c. Strict liability
   d. Master and Servant Acts

10. The _____ is a concept from business management that was first described and popularized by Michael Porter in his 1985 best-seller, Competitive Advantage: Creating and Sustaining Superior Performance.

    A _____ is a chain of activities. Products pass through all activities of the chain in order and at each activity the product gains some value. The chain of activities gives the products more added value than the sum of added values of all activities. It is important not to mix the concept of the _____ with the costs occurring throughout the activities.

    a. Customer relationship management
    b. Mass marketing
    c. Value chain
    d. Market development

11. _____ is the management of the flow of goods, information and other resources, including energy and people, between the point of origin and the point of consumption in order to meet the requirements of consumers (frequently, and originally, military organizations.) _____ involves the integration of information, transportation, inventory, warehousing, material-handling, and packaging, and occasionally security. _____ is a channel of the supply chain which adds the value of time and place utility.
    a. 28-hour day
    b. Third-party logistics
    c. Logistics
    d. 1990 Clean Air Act

12. _____ is an integrated communications-based process through which individuals and communities discover that existing and newly-identified needs and wants may be satisfied by the products and services of others.

Chapter 5. Strategic Management

23

_____ is defined by the American _____ Association as the activity, set of institutions, and processes for creating, communicating, delivering, and exchanging offerings that have value for customers, clients, partners, and society at large. The term developed from the original meaning which referred literally to going to market, as in shopping, or going to a market to buy or sell goods or services.

a. Disruptive technology
b. Customer relationship management
c. Market development
d. Marketing

13. _____ is an advertisement in which a particular product specifically mentions a competitor by name for the express purpose of showing why the competitor is inferior to the product naming it.

This should not be confused with parody advertisements, where a fictional product is being advertised for the purpose of poking fun at the particular advertisement, nor should it be confused with the use of a coined brand name for the purpose of comparing the product without actually naming an actual competitor. ('Wikipedia tastes better and is less filling than the Encyclopedia Galactica.')

In the 1980s, during what has been referred to as the cola wars, soft-drink manufacturer Pepsi ran a series of advertisements where people, caught on hidden camera, in a blind taste test, chose Pepsi over rival Coca-Cola.

a. 28-hour day
b. 33 Strategies of War
c. 1990 Clean Air Act
d. Comparative advertising

14. _____ is the strategic and coherent approach to the management of an organisation's most valued assets - the people working there who individually and collectively contribute to the achievement of the objectives of the business. The terms '_____' and 'human resources' (HR) have largely replaced the term 'personnel management' as a description of the processes involved in managing people in organizations. In simple sense, _____ means employing people, developing their resources, utilizing, maintaining and compensating their services in tune with the job and organizational requirement.

a. Job knowledge
b. Revolving door syndrome
c. Progressive discipline
d. Human resource management

15. _____ is the acquisition of goods and/or services at the best possible total cost of ownership, in the right quality and quantity, at the right time, in the right place and from the right source for the direct benefit or use of corporations, individuals generally via a contract. Simple _____ may involve nothing more than repeat purchasing. Complex _____ could involve finding long term partners - or even 'co-destiny' suppliers that might fundamentally commit one organization to another.
   a. Psychological pricing
   b. Sole proprietorship
   c. Procurement
   d. Golden parachute

16. A _____ is a process in which a potential employee is evaluated by an employer for prospective employment in their company, organization and was established in the late 16th century.

A _____ typically precedes the hiring decision, and is used to evaluate the candidate. The interview is usually preceded by the evaluation of submitted résumés from interested candidates, then selecting a small number of candidates for interviews.

   a. Split shift
   b. Job interview
   c. Supported employment
   d. Payrolling

17. _____ is an increasingly broadening term with which an organization, or other human system describes the combination of traditionally administrative personnel functions with acquisition and application of skills, knowledge and experience, Employee Relations and resource planning at various levels. The field draws upon concepts developed in Industrial/Organizational Psychology and System Theory. _____ has at least two related interpretations depending on context. The original usage derives from political economy and economics, where it was traditionally called labor, one of four factors of production although this perspective is changing as a function of new and ongoing research into more strategic approaches at national levels. This first usage is used more in terms of '_____ development', and can go beyond just organizations to the level of nations . The more traditional usage within corporations and businesses refers to the individuals within a firm or agency, and to the portion of the organization that deals with hiring, firing, training, and other personnel issues, typically referred to as '_____ management'.
   a. Human resources
   b. Bradford Factor
   c. Progressive discipline
   d. Human resource management

Chapter 5. Strategic Management

18. _____ is a strategic planning method used to evaluate the Strengths, Weaknesses, Opportunities, and Threats involved in a project or in a business venture. It involves specifying the objective of the business venture or project and identifying the internal and external factors that are favorable and unfavorable to achieving that objective. The technique is credited to Albert Humphrey, who led a convention at Stanford University in the 1960s and 1970s using data from Fortune 500 companies.
    a. Market share
    b. SWOT analysis
    c. Marketing
    d. Corporate image

19. _____ is a business management strategy, initially implemented by Motorola, that today enjoys widespread application in many sectors of industry.

    _____ seeks to improve the quality of process outputs by identifying and removing the causes of defects (errors) and variation in manufacturing and business processes. It uses a set of quality management methods, including statistical methods, and creates a special infrastructure of people within the organization ('Black Belts' etc.)

    a. Production line
    b. Takt time
    c. Six Sigma
    d. Theory of constraints

20. The phrase mergers and _____s refers to the aspect of corporate strategy, corporate finance and management dealing with the buying, selling and combining of different companies that can aid, finance, or help a growing company in a given industry grow rapidly without having to create another business entity.

    An _____, also known as a takeover or a buyout, is the buying of one company (the 'target') by another. An _____ may be friendly or hostile.

    a. AAAI
    b. Acquisition
    c. A Stake in the Outcome
    d. A4e

21. A _____ is a formal relationship between two or more parties to pursue a set of agreed upon goals or to meet a critical business need while remaining independent organizations.

Partners may provide the _____ with resources such as products, distribution channels, manufacturing capability, project funding, capital equipment, knowledge, expertise, or intellectual property. The alliance is a cooperation or collaboration which aims for a synergy where each partner hopes that the benefits from the alliance will be greater than those from individual efforts.

   a. Strategic alliance
   b. Golden parachute
   c. Process automation
   d. Farmshoring

22. An _____ is a person who has possession of an enterprise and assumes significant accountability for the inherent risks and the outcome. It is an ambitious leader who combines land, labor, and capital to create and market new goods or services. The term is a loanword from French and was first defined by the Irish economist Richard Cantillon.
   a. AAAI
   b. A4e
   c. A Stake in the Outcome
   d. Entrepreneur

Chapter 6. Planning

1. Procter is a surname, and may also refer to:

   - Bryan Waller Procter (pseud. Barry Cornwall), English poet
   - Goodwin Procter, American law firm
   - _____, consumer products multinational

   a. Downstream
   b. Master and Servant Acts
   c. Strict liability
   d. Procter ' Gamble

2. _____ is understood as a business unit within the overall corporate identity which is distinguishable from other business because it serves a defined external market where management can conduct strategic planning in relation to products and markets. When companies become really large, they are best thought of as being composed of a number of businesses (or _____s.)

   In the broader domain of strategic management, the phrase '_____' came into use in the 1960s, largely as a result of General Electric's many units.

   a. Strategic business unit
   b. Strategic drift
   c. Switching cost
   d. Strategic group

3. _____ is one of the managerial functions like planning, organizing, staffing and directing. It is an important function because it helps to check the errors and to take the corrective action so that deviation from standards are minimized and stated goals of the organization are achieved in desired manner. According to modern concepts, _____ is a foreseeing action whereas earlier concept of _____ was used only when errors were detected. _____ in management means setting standards, measuring actual performance and taking corrective action.

   a. Schedule of reinforcement
   b. Control
   c. Turnover
   d. Decision tree pruning

4. _____ is the process of comparing the cost, cycle time, productivity, or quality of a specific process or method to another that is widely considered to be an industry standard or best practice. Essentially, _____ provides a snapshot of the performance of your business and helps you understand where you are in relation to a particular standard. The result is often a business case for making changes in order to make improvements.

a. Complementors
b. Benchmarking
c. Competitive heterogeneity
d. Cost leadership

5. A _____ is a plan devised for a specific situation when things could go wrong. _____s are often devised by governments or businesses who want to be prepared for anything that could happen. They are sometimes known as 'Back-up plans', 'Worst-case scenario plans' or 'Plan B'.
   a. 1990 Clean Air Act
   b. Contingency plan
   c. 33 Strategies of War
   d. 28-hour day

6. A _____ is a process in which a potential employee is evaluated by an employer for prospective employment in their company, organization and was established in the late 16th century.

A _____ typically precedes the hiring decision, and is used to evaluate the candidate. The interview is usually preceded by the evaluation of submitted résumés from interested candidates, then selecting a small number of candidates for interviews.

   a. Split shift
   b. Payrolling
   c. Supported employment
   d. Job interview

7. _____ is the process of estimation in unknown situations. Prediction is a similar, but more general term. Both can refer to estimation of time series, cross-sectional or longitudinal data.
   a. Forecasting
   b. 28-hour day
   c. 1990 Clean Air Act
   d. 33 Strategies of War

8. A _____ is a type of bar chart that illustrates a project schedule. _____s illustrate the start and finish dates of the terminal elements and summary elements of a project. Terminal elements and summary elements comprise the work breakdown structure of the project.

Chapter 6. Planning

a. 33 Strategies of War
b. 1990 Clean Air Act
c. 28-hour day
d. Gantt chart

9. _____ is a concept in ethics with several meanings. It is often used synonymously with such concepts as responsibility, answerability, enforcement, blameworthiness, liability and other terms associated with the expectation of account-giving. As an aspect of governance, it has been central to discussions related to problems in both the public and private (corporation) worlds.
   a. Usury
   b. A Stake in the Outcome
   c. A4e
   d. Accountability

10. In game theory, an _____ is a set of moves or strategies taken by the players, or their payoffs resulting from the actions or strategies taken by all players. The two are complementary in that given knowledge of the set of strategies of all players, the final state of the game is known, as are any relevant payoffs. In a game where chance or a random event is involved, the _____ is not known from only the set of strategies, but is only realized when the random event(s) are realized.
   a. A4e
   b. AAAI
   c. A Stake in the Outcome
   d. Outcome

11. _____ generally refers to a list of all planned expenses and revenues. It is a plan for saving and spending. A _____ is an important concept in microeconomics, which uses a _____ line to illustrate the trade-offs between two or more goods.
   a. 1990 Clean Air Act
   b. Budget
   c. 33 Strategies of War
   d. 28-hour day

12. _____ involves establishing specific, measurable and time-targeted objectives. Work on the theory of goal-setting suggests that it's an effective tool for making progress by ensuring that participants in a group with a common goal are clearly aware of what is expected from them if an objective is to be achieved. On a personal level, setting goals is a process that allows people to specify then work towards their own objectives - most commonly with financial or career-based goals.

a. Digital strategy
b. Catfish effect
c. Goal setting
d. Resource-based view

13. _____ has been described as the 'process of social influence in which one person can enlist the aid and support of others in the accomplishment of a common task' . A definition more inclusive of followers comes from Alan Keith of Genentech who said '_____ is ultimately about creating a way for people to contribute to making something extraordinary happen.'

_____ is one of the most salient aspects of the organizational context. However, defining _____ has been challenging.

a. Leadership
b. 1990 Clean Air Act
c. 28-hour day
d. Situational leadership

Chapter 7. Organizational Structure and Design

1. An _____, or organogram(me)) is a diagram that shows the structure of an organization and the relationships and relative ranks of its parts and positions/jobs. The term is also used for similar diagrams, for example ones showing the different elements of a field of knowledge or a group of languages. The French Encyclopédie had one of the first _____s of knowledge in general.
   a. A4e
   b. Organizational chart
   c. AAAI
   d. A Stake in the Outcome

2. An _____ is a mostly hierarchical concept of subordination of entities that collaborate and contribute to serve one common aim.

   Organizations are a variant of clustered entities. The structure of an organization is usually set up in many a styles, dependent on their objectives and ambience.

   a. Organizational development
   b. Open shop
   c. Organizational structure
   d. Informal organization

3. _____ is a dynamic of being mutually and physically responsible to and sharing a common set of principles with others. This concept differs distinctly from 'dependence' in that an interdependent relationship implies that all participants are emotionally, economically, ecologically and or morally 'interdependent.' Some people advocate freedom or independence as a sort of ultimate good; others do the same with devotion to one's family, community, or society. _____ recognizes the truth in each position and weaves them together.
   a. A4e
   b. AAAI
   c. Interdependence
   d. A Stake in the Outcome

4. A _____ is a set of instructions having the force of a directive, covering those features of operations that lend themselves to a definite or standardized procedure without loss of effectiveness. Standard Operating Policies and Procedures can be effective catalysts to drive performance improvement and improving organizational results.
   a. 1990 Clean Air Act
   b. Standard operating procedure
   c. Risk-benefit analysis
   d. Longitudinal study

Chapter 7. Organizational Structure and Design

5. _____ is the process of estimation in unknown situations. Prediction is a similar, but more general term. Both can refer to estimation of time series, cross-sectional or longitudinal data.
   a. 33 Strategies of War
   b. 28-hour day
   c. 1990 Clean Air Act
   d. Forecasting

6. _____ is the self-government of a nation, country or some portion thereof, generally exercising sovereignty.

The term _____ is used in contrast to subjugation, which refers to a region as a 'territory' --subject to the political and military control of an external government. The word is sometimes used in a weaker sense to contrast with hegemony, the indirect control of one nation by another, more powerful nation.

   a. AAAI
   b. A4e
   c. A Stake in the Outcome
   d. Independence

7. _____ is a term originating in military organization theory, but now used more commonly in business management, particularly human resource management. _____ refers to the number of subordinates a supervisor has.

In the hierarchical business organization of the past it was not uncommon to see average spans of 1 to 10 or even less. That is, one manager supervised ten employees on average.

   a. CIFMS
   b. Mentoring
   c. Senior management
   d. Span of control

8. The _____ is a standardized, on-scene, all-hazard incident management concept. It is a management protocol originally designed for emergency management agencies in the United States which was later federalized there. It has since been adopted by agencies in other countries.
   a. A4e
   b. AAAI
   c. A Stake in the Outcome
   d. Incident Command Structure

Chapter 7. Organizational Structure and Design

9. _____ is one of the managerial functions like planning, organizing, staffing and directing. It is an important function because it helps to check the errors and to take the corrective action so that deviation from standards are minimized and stated goals of the organization are achieved in desired manner. According to modern concepts, _____ is a foreseeing action whereas earlier concept of _____ was used only when errors were detected. _____ in management means setting standards, measuring actual performance and taking corrective action.
   a. Control
   b. Decision tree pruning
   c. Turnover
   d. Schedule of reinforcement

10. _____ (known as horizontal organization) refers to an organizational structure with few or no levels of intervening management between staff and managers. The idea is that well-trained workers will be more productive when they are more directly involved in the decision making process, rather than closely supervised by many layers of management.

    This structure is generally possible only in smaller organizations or individual units within larger organizations.

   a. 33 Strategies of War
   b. 1990 Clean Air Act
   c. 28-hour day
   d. Flat organization

11. The _____ is the interlocking social structure that governs how people work together in practice. It is the aggregate of behaviors, interactions, norms, personal and professional connections through which work gets done and relationships are built among people who share a common organizational affiliation or cluster of affiliations. It consists of a dynamic set of personal relationships, social networks, communities of common interest, and emotional sources of motivation. The _____ evolves organically and spontaneously in response to changes in the work environment, the flux of people through its porous boundaries, and the complex social dynamics of its members.
   a. Organizational effectiveness
   b. Open shop
   c. Union shop
   d. Informal organization

12. _____s are parts of a corporation that directly add to its profit.

A _____ manager is held accountable for both revenues, and costs (expenses), and therefore, profits. What this means in terms of managerial responsibilities is that the manager has to drive the sales revenue generating activities which leads to cash inflows and at the same time control the cost (cash outflows) causing activities.

a. Factory overhead
b. Process costing
c. Customer profitability
d. Profit center

13. A _____ is a relatively new executive level position at a corporation, company, organization typically reporting directly to the CEO or board of directors. The _____ is responsible for a brand's image, experience, and promise, and propagating it throughout all aspects of the company. The brand officer oversees marketing, advertising, design, public relations and customer service departments.

   a. Chief executive officer
   b. Director of communications
   c. Purchasing manager
   d. Chief brand officer

14. _____ is subcontracting a process, such as product design or manufacturing, to a third-party company. The decision to outsource is often made in the interest of lowering cost or making better use of time and energy costs, redirecting or conserving energy directed at the competencies of a particular business, or to make more efficient use of land, labor, capital, (information) technology and resources. _____ became part of the business lexicon during the 1980s.

   a. Outsourcing
   b. Operant conditioning
   c. Opinion leadership
   d. Unemployment insurance

15. Procter is a surname, and may also refer to:

   - Bryan Waller Procter (pseud. Barry Cornwall), English poet
   - Goodwin Procter, American law firm
   - _____, consumer products multinational

a. Strict liability
b. Master and Servant Acts
c. Downstream
d. Procter ' Gamble

Chapter 8. Managing Diverse Human Resources

1. _____ is the strategic and coherent approach to the management of an organisation's most valued assets - the people working there who individually and collectively contribute to the achievement of the objectives of the business. The terms '_____' and 'human resources' (HR) have largely replaced the term 'personnel management' as a description of the processes involved in managing people in organizations. In simple sense, _____ means employing people, developing their resources, utilizing, maintaining and compensating their services in tune with the job and organizational requirement.
   a. Human resource management
   b. Job knowledge
   c. Revolving door syndrome
   d. Progressive discipline

2. _____ is an increasingly broadening term with which an organization, or other human system describes the combination of traditionally administrative personnel functions with acquisition and application of skills, knowledge and experience, Employee Relations and resource planning at various levels. The field draws upon concepts developed in Industrial/Organizational Psychology and System Theory. _____ has at least two related interpretations depending on context. The original usage derives from political economy and economics, where it was traditionally called labor, one of four factors of production although this perspective is changing as a function of new and ongoing research into more strategic approaches at national levels. This first usage is used more in terms of '_____ development', and can go beyond just organizations to the level of nations. The more traditional usage within corporations and businesses refers to the individuals within a firm or agency, and to the portion of the organization that deals with hiring, firing, training, and other personnel issues, typically referred to as '_____ management'.
   a. Progressive discipline
   b. Bradford Factor
   c. Human resources
   d. Human resource management

3. In economics, _____ is the desire to own something and the ability to pay for it. The term _____ signifies the ability or the willingness to buy a particular commodity at a given point of time.
   a. 28-hour day
   b. 1990 Clean Air Act
   c. Demand
   d. 33 Strategies of War

4. _____ is one of the managerial functions like planning, organizing, staffing and directing. It is an important function because it helps to check the errors and to take the corrective action so that deviation from standards are minimized and stated goals of the organization are achieved in desired manner. According to modern concepts, _____ is a foreseeing action whereas earlier concept of _____ was used only when errors were detected. _____ in management means setting standards, measuring actual performance and taking corrective action.

Chapter 8. Managing Diverse Human Resources

   a. Turnover
   b. Decision tree pruning
   c. Schedule of reinforcement
   d. Control

5. _____ is the process of estimation in unknown situations. Prediction is a similar, but more general term. Both can refer to estimation of time series, cross-sectional or longitudinal data.
   a. 1990 Clean Air Act
   b. Forecasting
   c. 28-hour day
   d. 33 Strategies of War

6. The _____ captures an expanded spectrum of values and criteria for measuring organizational success: economic, ecological and social. With the ratification of the United Nations and ICLEI _____ standard for urban and community accounting in early 2007, this became the dominant approach to public sector full cost accounting. Similar UN standards apply to natural capital and human capital measurement to assist in measurements required by _____, e.g. the ecoBudget standard for reporting ecological footprint.
   a. 28-hour day
   b. 1990 Clean Air Act
   c. 33 Strategies of War
   d. Triple bottom line

7. _____ refers to various methodologies for analyzing the requirements of a job.

The general purpose of _____ is to document the requirements of a job and the work performed. Job and task analysis is performed as a basis for later improvements, including: definition of a job domain; describing a job; developing performance appraisals, selection systems, promotion criteria, training needs assessment, and compensation plans.

   a. Management process
   b. Work design
   c. Job analysis
   d. Hersey-Blanchard situational theory

8. A _____ is a list of the general tasks and responsibilities of a position. Typically, it also includes to whom the position reports, specifications such as the qualifications needed by the person in the job, salary range for the position, etc. A _____ is usually developed by conducting a job analysis, which includes examining the tasks and sequences of tasks necessary to perform the job.

a. Recruitment advertising
b. Recruitment
c. Recruitment Process Insourcing
d. Job description

9. _____ is subcontracting a process, such as product design or manufacturing, to a third-party company. The decision to outsource is often made in the interest of lowering cost or making better use of time and energy costs, redirecting or conserving energy directed at the competencies of a particular business, or to make more efficient use of land, labor, capital, (information) technology and resources. _____ became part of the business lexicon during the 1980s.
   a. Opinion leadership
   b. Unemployment insurance
   c. Operant conditioning
   d. Outsourcing

10. _____ is an advertisement in which a particular product specifically mentions a competitor by name for the express purpose of showing why the competitor is inferior to the product naming it.

This should not be confused with parody advertisements, where a fictional product is being advertised for the purpose of poking fun at the particular advertisement, nor should it be confused with the use of a coined brand name for the purpose of comparing the product without actually naming an actual competitor. ('Wikipedia tastes better and is less filling than the Encyclopedia Galactica.')

In the 1980s, during what has been referred to as the cola wars, soft-drink manufacturer Pepsi ran a series of advertisements where people, caught on hidden camera, in a blind taste test, chose Pepsi over rival Coca-Cola.

   a. 33 Strategies of War
   b. 1990 Clean Air Act
   c. 28-hour day
   d. Comparative advertising

11. A _____ is a provisional group of workers who work for an organization on a non-permanent basis independent professionals, temporary contract workers, independent contractors or consultants. _____ Management is the strategic approach to managing an organization's _____ in a way that it reduces the company's cost in the management of contingent employees and mitigates the company's risk in employing them.

Chapter 8. Managing Diverse Human Resources

According to the US Bureau of Labor Statistics, the nontraditional workforce includes 'multiple job holders, contingent and part-time workers, and people in alternative work arrangements.' These workers currently represent a substantial portion of the U.S. workforce, and 'nearly four out of five employers, in establishments of all sizes and industries, use some form of nontraditional staffing.' 'People in alternative work arrangements' includes independent contractors, employees of contract companies, workers who are on call, and temporary workers.

   a. 1990 Clean Air Act
   b. Contingent workforce
   c. 33 Strategies of War
   d. 28-hour day

12. _____ is a form of communication that typically attempts to persuade potential customers to purchase or to consume more of a particular brand of product or service. 'While now central to the contemporary global economy and the reproduction of global production networks, it is only quite recently that _____ has been more than a marginal influence on patterns of sales and production. The formation of modern _____ was intimately bound up with the emergence of new forms of monopoly capitalism around the end of the 19th and beginning of the 20th century as one element in corporate strategies to create, organize and where possible control markets, especially for mass produced consumer goods.
   a. Advertising
   b. AAAI
   c. A Stake in the Outcome
   d. A4e

13. _____ is a contract between two parties, one being the employer and the other being the employee. An employee may be defined as: 'A person in the service of another under any contract of hire, express or implied, oral or written, where the employer has the power or right to control and direct the employee in the material details of how the work is to be performed.' Black's Law Dictionary page 471 (5th ed. 1979.)
   a. Employment rate
   b. Exit interview
   c. Employment counsellor
   d. Employment

14. _____ is an internal recruitment method employed by organisations to identify potential candidates from their existing employees social networks. An _____ scheme encourages a company's existing employees to select and recruit the suitable candidates from their social networks. As a reward, the employer typically pays the referring employee a referral bonus.

a. Internet recruiting
b. Employee referral
c. Employment agency
d. Executive search

15. A _____ is a quantitative research method commonly employed in survey research. The aim of this approach is to ensure that each interviewee is presented with exactly the same questions in the same order. This ensures that answers can be reliably aggregated and that comparisons can be made with confidence between sample subgroups or between different survey periods.
    a. Mystery shoppers
    b. Questionnaire construction
    c. Questionnaire
    d. Structured interview

16. A _____ or background investigation is the process of looking up and compiling criminal records, commercial records and financial records (in certain instances such as employment screening) of an individual.

    _____s are often requested by employers on job candidates, especially on candidates seeking a position that requires high security or a position of trust, such as in a school, hospital, financial institution, airport, and government (including law enforcement and military.) These checks are traditionally administered by a government agency for a nominal fee, but can also be administered by private companies.

    a. Malcolm Baldrige National Quality Award
    b. Time and attendance
    c. Labour productivity
    d. Background check

17. A _____ is a professional who provides advice in a particular area of expertise such as management, accountancy, the environment, entertainment, technology, law, human resources, marketing, medicine, finance, economics, public affairs, communication, engineering, sound system design, graphic design, or waste management.

    A _____ is usually an expert or a professional in a specific field and has a wide knowledge of the subject matter. A _____ usually works for a consultancy firm or is self-employed, and engages with multiple and changing clients.

a. 28-hour day
b. 1990 Clean Air Act
c. Consultant
d. 33 Strategies of War

18. _____ is an approach to management development where an individual is moved through a schedule of assignments designed to give him or her a breadth of exposure to the entire operation.

_____ is also practiced to allow qualified employees to gain more insights into the processes of a company, and to reduce boredom and increase job satisfaction through job variation.

The term _____ can also mean the scheduled exchange of persons in offices, especially in public offices, prior to the end of incumbency or the legislative period.

a. 28-hour day
b. Job rotation
c. 33 Strategies of War
d. 1990 Clean Air Act

19. There are two types of _____ relationships: formal and informal. Informal relationships develop on their own between partners. Formal _____, on the other hand, refers to assigned relationships, often associated with organizational _____ programs designed to promote employee development or to assist at-risk children and youth.

a. Human resource management system
b. Fix it twice
c. Real Property Administrator
d. Mentoring

20. In organizational development (OD), _____ is the application of Socio-Technical Systems principles and techniques to the humanization of work.

The aims of _____ to improved job satisfaction, to improved through-put, to improved quality and to reduced employee problems, e.g., grievances, absenteeism.

Under scientific management people would be directed by reason and the problems of industrial unrest would be appropriately (i.e., scientifically) addressed.

Chapter 8. Managing Diverse Human Resources 41

   a. Path-goal theory
   b. Management process
   c. Graduate recruitment
   d. Work design

21. _____ is a business management strategy, initially implemented by Motorola, that today enjoys widespread application in many sectors of industry.

_____ seeks to improve the quality of process outputs by identifying and removing the causes of defects (errors) and variation in manufacturing and business processes. It uses a set of quality management methods, including statistical methods, and creates a special infrastructure of people within the organization ('Black Belts' etc.)

   a. Six Sigma
   b. Takt time
   c. Theory of constraints
   d. Production line

22. In psychology research on behaviorism, _____ are scales used to report performance. _____ are normally presented vertically with scale points ranging from five to nine.

It is an appraisal method that aims to combine the benefits of narratives, critical incident incidents, and quantified ratings by anchoring a quantified scale with specific narrative examples of good or poor performance.

   a. Behaviorally anchored rating scales
   b. 33 Strategies of War
   c. 1990 Clean Air Act
   d. 28-hour day

23. A _____ is a set of categories designed to elicit information about a quantitative or a qualitative attribute. In the social sciences, common examples are the Likert scale and 1-10 _____s in which a person selects the number which is considered to reflect the perceived quality of a product.

A _____ is an instrument that requires the rater to assign the rated object that have numerals assigned to them.

a. Thurstone scale
b. Polytomous Rasch model
c. Spearman-Brown prediction formula
d. Rating scale

24. In human resources or industrial/organizational psychology, _____' 'multisource feedback,' or 'multisource assessment,' is feedback that comes from all around an employee. '360' refers to the 360 degrees in a circle, with an individual figuratively in the center of the circle. Feedback is provided by subordinates, peers, and supervisors.
    a. Job knowledge
    b. Personnel management
    c. Revolving door syndrome
    d. 360-degree feedback

25. _____ describes the situation when output from (or information about the result of) an event or phenomenon in the past will influence the same event/phenomenon in the present or future. When an event is part of a chain of cause-and-effect that forms a circuit or loop, then the event is said to 'feed back' into itself.

_____ is also a synonym for:

- _____ signal; the information about the initial event that is the basis for subsequent modification of the event.
- _____ loop; the causal path that leads from the initial generation of the _____ signal to the subsequent modification of the event.

_____ is a mechanism, process or signal that is looped back to control a system within itself. Such a loop is called a _____ loop.

a. Feedback loop
b. 1990 Clean Air Act
c. Positive feedback
d. Feedback

26. In economics and sociology, an _____ is any factor (financial or non-financial) that enables or motivates a particular course of action, or counts as a reason for preferring one choice to the alternatives. It is an expectation that encourages people to behave in a certain way. Since human beings are purposeful creatures, the study of _____ structures is central to the study of all economic activity (both in terms of individual decision-making and in terms of co-operation and competition within a larger institutional structure.)

Chapter 8. Managing Diverse Human Resources 43

a. AAAI
b. A4e
c. A Stake in the Outcome
d. Incentive

27. An _____ is a formal scheme used to promote or encourage specific actions or behavior by a specific group of people during a defined period of time. _____s are particularly used in business management to motivate employees, and in sales in order to attract and retain customers. The scientific literature also refers to this concept as Pay for Performance.

a. A4e
b. A Stake in the Outcome
c. AAAI
d. Incentive program

28. In decision theory and estimation theory, the _____ of an estimator, $\hat{\theta}$, of an unknown parameter of the distribution, θ, is the expected value of the loss function

$$R(\theta, \hat{\theta}) = \mathbb{E}_\theta L(\theta, \hat{\theta}) = \int L(\theta, \hat{\theta})\, dP_\theta.$$

where dP_θ is a probability measure parametrized by θ.

- For a scalar parameter θ and a quadratic loss function,

$$L(\theta, \hat{\theta}) = (\theta - \hat{\theta})^2$$

  the _____ function becomes the mean squared error of the estimate,

$$R(\theta, \hat{\theta}) = E_\theta (\theta - \hat{\theta})^2$$

- In density estimation, the unknown parameter is probability density itself. The loss function is typically chosen to be a norm in an appropriate function space. For example, for L^2 norm,

$$L(f, \hat{f}) = \|f - \hat{f}\|_2^2$$

  the _____ function becomes the mean integrated squared error

$$R(f, \hat{f}) = E\|f - \hat{f}\|^2$$

a. Risk aversion
b. Linear model
c. Financial modeling
d. Risk

29. In ethology, _____ is an effect whereby individual people may tend to adjust their behaviour in response to perceived changes in risk. It is seen as self-evident that individuals will tend to behave in a more cautious manner if their perception of risk or danger increases. Another way of stating this is that individuals will behave less cautiously in situations where they feel 'safer' or more protected.
a. 28-hour day
b. 33 Strategies of War
c. Risk compensation
d. 1990 Clean Air Act

30. _____ is a term defined by the Oxford English Dictionary as an individual's 'course or progress through life '. It is usually considered to pertain to remunerative work (and sometimes also formal education.)

The etymology of the term is somewhat ironic in that it comes from the Latin word carrera, which means race .

a. Nursing shortage
b. Career planning
c. Spatial mismatch
d. Career

31. _____ is the temporary suspension or permanent termination of employment of an employee or (more commonly) a group of employees for business reasons, such as the decision that certain positions are no longer necessary or a business slow-down or interruption in work. Originally the term '_____' referred exclusively to a temporary interruption in work, as when factory work cyclically falls off. However, in recent times the term can also refer to the permanent elimination of a position.

a. Wrongful dismissal
b. Retirement
c. Termination of employment
d. Layoff

32. The field of _____ looks at the relationship between management and workers, particularly groups of workers represented by a union.

_____ is an important factor in analyzing 'varieties of capitalism', such as neocorporatism, social democracy, and neoliberalism

a. Overtime
b. Organizational effectiveness
c. Informal organization
d. Industrial relations

33. The 'business case for _____', theorizes that in a global marketplace, a company that employs a diverse workforce (both men and women, people of many generations, people from ethnically and racially diverse backgrounds etc.) is better able to understand the demographics of the marketplace it serves and is thus better equipped to thrive in that marketplace than a company that has a more limited range of employee demographics.

An additional corollary suggests that a company that supports the _____ of its workforce can also improve employee satisfaction, productivity and retention.

a. Diversity
b. Virtual team
c. Trademark
d. Kanban

Chapter 8. Managing Diverse Human Resources

34. In economics, the term _____ refers to situations where the advancement of a qualified person within the hierarchy of an organization is stopped at a lower level because of some form of discrimination, most commonly sexism or racism, but since the term was coined, '_____' has also come to describe the limited advancement of the deaf, blind, disabled, aged and sexual minorities. It is an unofficial, invisible barrier that prevents women and minorities from advancing in businesses.

This situation is referred to as a 'ceiling' as there is a limitation blocking upward advancement, and 'glass' (transparent) because the limitation is not immediately apparent and is normally an unwritten and unofficial policy. This invisible barrier continues to exist, even though there are no explicit obstacles keeping minorities from acquiring advanced job positions - there are no advertisements that specifically say 'no minorities hired at this establishment', nor are there any formal orders that say 'minorities are not qualified' - but they do lie beneath the surface.

   a. 28-hour day
   b. 33 Strategies of War
   c. 1990 Clean Air Act
   d. Glass ceiling

35. _____ or _____ data refers to selected population characteristics as used in government, marketing or opinion research, or the _____ profiles used in such research. Note the distinction from the term 'demography' Commonly-used _____s include race, age, income, disabilities, mobility (in terms of travel time to work or number of vehicles available), educational attainment, home ownership, employment status, and even location.
   a. Abraham Harold Maslow
   b. Demographic
   c. Affiliation
   d. Adam Smith

36. The _____ is the labour pool in employment. It is generally used to describe those working for a single company or industry, but can also apply to a geographic region like a city, country, state, etc. The term generally excludes the employers or management, and implies those involved in manual labour.
   a. Division of labour
   b. Pink-collar worker
   c. Work-life balance
   d. Workforce

37. _____ is unwelcome harassment of a sexual nature, or based upon the receiving party's sex or gender. In some contexts or circumstances, _____ may be illegal. It includes a range of behavior from seemingly mild transgressions and annoyances to actual sexual abuse or sexual assault.

Chapter 8. Managing Diverse Human Resources

a. Hypernorms
b. 28-hour day
c. 1990 Clean Air Act
d. Sexual harassment

38.

The terms _____ and positive action refer to policies that take race, ethnicity, or gender into consideration in an attempt to promote equal opportunity. The focus of such policies ranges from employment and education to public contracting and health programs. The impetus towards _____ is twofold: to maximize diversity in all levels of society, along with its presumed benefits, and to redress perceived disadvantages due to overt, institutional, or involuntary discrimination.

a. Affiliation
b. Affirmative action
c. Abraham Harold Maslow
d. Adam Smith

39. The _____ of 1967, Pub. L. No. 90-202, 81 Stat. 602 (Dec. 15, 1967), codified as Chapter 14 of Title 29 of the United States Code, 29 U.S.C. § 621 through 29 U.S.C. § 634 (ADEA), prohibits employment discrimination against persons 40 years of age or older in the United States). The law also sets standards for pensions and benefits provided by employers and requires that information about the needs of older workers be provided to the general public.

a. Extra time
b. Unemployment and Farm Relief Act
c. Undue hardship
d. Age Discrimination in Employment Act

40. The _____ of 1990 (ADA) is the short title of United States (Pub.L. 101-336, 104 Stat. 327, enacted July 26, 1990), codified at 42 U.S.C. § 12101 et seq. It was signed into law on July 26, 1990, by President George H. W. Bush, and later amended with changes effective January 1, 2009. The ADA is a wide-ranging civil rights law that prohibits, under certain circumstances, discrimination based on disability. It affords similar protections against discrimination to Americans with disabilities as the Civil Rights Act of 1964,

a. Employment discrimination
b. Equal Pay Act of 1963
c. Australian labour law
d. Americans with Disabilities Act

Chapter 8. Managing Diverse Human Resources

41. The _____ 1970 is an Act of the United Kingdom Parliament which prohibits any less favourable treatment between men and women in terms of pay and conditions of employment. It came into force on 29 December 1975. The term pay is interpreted in a broad sense to include, on top of wages, things like holidays, pension rights, company perks and some kinds of bonuses.
    a. Oncale v. Sundowner Offshore Services
    b. Architectural Barriers Act of 1968
    c. Equal Pay Act
    d. Australian labour law

42. The _____ is a United States labor law allowing an employee to take unpaid leave due to a serious health condition that makes the employee unable to perform his job or to care for a sick family member or to care for a new son or daughter (including by birth, adoption or foster care.) The bill was among the first signed into law by President Bill Clinton in his first term.
    a. Sarbanes-Oxley Act of 2002
    b. Harvester Judgment
    c. Contributory negligence
    d. Family and Medical Leave Act of 1993

43. The U.S. _____ of 1973 prohibits discrimination on the basis of disability in programs conducted by Federal agencies, in programs receiving Federal financial assistance, in Federal employment, and in the employment practices of Federal contractors. The standards for determining employment discrimination under the _____ are the same as those used in title I of the Americans with Disabilities Act.

There are four key sections of the Act.

    a. Rehabilitation Act
    b. 1990 Clean Air Act
    c. 33 Strategies of War
    d. 28-hour day

44. A _____ is a process in which a potential employee is evaluated by an employer for prospective employment in their company, organization and was established in the late 16th century.

A _____ typically precedes the hiring decision, and is used to evaluate the candidate. The interview is usually preceded by the evaluation of submitted résumés from interested candidates, then selecting a small number of candidates for interviews.

a. Payrolling
b. Split shift
c. Supported employment
d. Job interview

45. _____ in its literal sense is the process of transformation of local or regional phenomena into global ones. It can be described as a process by which the people of the world are unified into a single society and function together.

This process is a combination of economic, technological, sociocultural and political forces.

a. Cost Management
b. Histogram
c. Collaborative Planning, Forecasting and Replenishment
d. Globalization

Chapter 9. Leadership

1. _____ has been described as the 'process of social influence in which one person can enlist the aid and support of others in the accomplishment of a common task' . A definition more inclusive of followers comes from Alan Keith of Genentech who said '_____ is ultimately about creating a way for people to contribute to making something extraordinary happen.'

_____ is one of the most salient aspects of the organizational context. However, defining _____ has been challenging.

a. 28-hour day
b. Situational leadership
c. 1990 Clean Air Act
d. Leadership

2. _____ refers to the movement of cash into or out of a business or financial product. It is usually measured during a specified, finite period of time. Measurement of _____ can be used

- to determine a project's rate of return or value. The time of _____s into and out of projects are used as inputs in financial models such as internal rate of return, and net present value.
- to determine problems with a business's liquidity. Being profitable does not necessarily mean being liquid. A company can fail because of a shortage of cash, even while profitable.
- as an alternate measure of a business's profits when it is believed that accrual accounting concepts do not represent economic realities. For example, a company may be notionally profitable but generating little operational cash (as may be the case for a company that barters its products rather than selling for cash.) In such a case, the company may be deriving additional operating cash by issuing shares evaluating default risk, re-investment requirements, etc.

_____ is a generic term used differently depending on the context. It may be defined by users for their own purposes.

a. Gross profit margin
b. Sweat equity
c. Gross profit
d. Cash flow

3. There are two types of _____ relationships: formal and informal. Informal relationships develop on their own between partners. Formal _____, on the other hand, refers to assigned relationships, often associated with organizational _____ programs designed to promote employee development or to assist at-risk children and youth.
a. Human resource management system
b. Fix it twice
c. Real Property Administrator
d. Mentoring

Chapter 9. Leadership

4. _____ refers to increasing the spiritual, political, social or economic strength of individuals and communities. It often involves the empowered developing confidence in their own capacities.

The term Human _____ covers a vast landscape of meanings, interpretations, definitions and disciplines ranging from psychology and philosophy to the highly commercialized Self-Help industry and Motivational sciences.

   a. AAAI
   b. A Stake in the Outcome
   c. A4e
   d. Empowerment

5. _____ , often measured as an _____ Quotient (EQ), is a term that describes the ability, capacity, skill or (in the case of the trait _____ model) a self-perceived ability, to identify, assess, and manage the emotions of one's self, of others, and of groups. Different models have been proposed for the definition of _____ and disagreement exists as to how the term should be used. Despite these disagreements, which are often highly technical, the ability _____ and trait _____ models (but not the mixed models) are enjoying considerable support in the literature and have successful applications in many different domains.
   a. AAAI
   b. A4e
   c. A Stake in the Outcome
   d. Emotional intelligence

6. The _____ captures an expanded spectrum of values and criteria for measuring organizational success: economic, ecological and social. With the ratification of the United Nations and ICLEI _____ standard for urban and community accounting in early 2007, this became the dominant approach to public sector full cost accounting. Similar UN standards apply to natural capital and human capital measurement to assist in measurements required by _____, e.g. the ecoBudget standard for reporting ecological footprint.
   a. 33 Strategies of War
   b. 1990 Clean Air Act
   c. Triple bottom line
   d. 28-hour day

7. _____ is a leadership style that defines as leadership that creates voluble and positive change in the followers. A transformational leader focuses on 'transforming' others to help each other, to look out for each other, be encouraging, harmonious, and look out for the organization as a whole. In this leadership, the leader enhances the motivation, moral and performance of his follower group.

a. SESAMO
b. Polynomial conjoint measurement
c. Strong-Campbell Interest Inventory
d. Transformational leadership

8. _____ is a term used to classify a group leadership theories that inquire the interactions between leaders and followers. A transactional leader focuses more on a series of 'transactions'. This person is interested in looking out for oneself, having exchange benefits with their subordinates and clarify a sense of duty with rewards and punishments to reach goals.
   a. 33 Strategies of War
   b. 28-hour day
   c. Transactional leadership
   d. 1990 Clean Air Act

9. _____ is one of the managerial functions like planning, organizing, staffing and directing. It is an important function because it helps to check the errors and to take the corrective action so that deviation from standards are minimized and stated goals of the organization are achieved in desired manner. According to modern concepts, _____ is a foreseeing action whereas earlier concept of _____ was used only when errors were detected. _____ in management means setting standards, measuring actual performance and taking corrective action.
   a. Decision tree pruning
   b. Turnover
   c. Schedule of reinforcement
   d. Control

10. Contingency leadership theory in organizational studies is a type of leadership theory, leadership style, and leadership model that presumes that different leadership styles are contingent to different situations. It is also referred as _____ Â® theory although, as originally convened, the situational theory term is much more restrictive. The original situational theory argues that the best type of leadership is totally determined by the situational variables. Currently there are many styles of leadership.
   a. Situational Leadership
   b. 1990 Clean Air Act
   c. 28-hour day
   d. Situational theory

11. _____ is a class of behavioural theory that claims that there is no best way to organize a corporation, to lead a company, or to make decisions. Instead, the optimal course of action is contingent (dependant) upon the internal and external situation. Several contingency approaches were developed concurrently in the late 1960s.

a. Capability management
b. Distributed management
c. Commercial management
d. Contingency theory

12. The _____ is a leadership theory in the field of organizational studies developed by Robert House in 1971 and revised in 1996. The theory that a leader's behavior is contingent to the satisfaction, motivation and performance of subordinates. The revised version also argues that the leader engage in behaviors that complement subordinate's abilities and compensate for deficiencies.
a. Corporate Culture
b. Human relations
c. Path-goal theory
d. Sociotechnical systems

Chapter 10. Motivation

1. _____ is a term that has been used in various psychology theories, often in slightly different ways (e.g., Goldstein, Maslow, Rogers.) The term was originally introduced by the organismic theorist Kurt Goldstein for the motive to realise all of one's potentialities. In his view, it is the master motive--indeed, the only real motive a person has, all others being merely manifestations of it.
   a. 28-hour day
   b. Self-actualization
   c. 1990 Clean Air Act
   d. 33 Strategies of War

2. Clayton Paul Alderfer is an American psychologist who further expanded Maslow's hierarchy of needs by categorizing the hierarchy into his _____ Alderfer categorized the lower order needs (Physiological and Safety) into the Existence category. He fit Maslow's interpersonal love and esteem needs into the relatedness category. The growth category contained the Self Actualization and self esteem needs.

   Alderfer also proposed a regression theory to go along with the _____. He said that when needs in a higher category are not met then individuals redouble the efforts invested in a lower category need.

   a. Abraham Harold Maslow
   b. Alvin Neill Jackson
   c. Adam Smith
   d. ERG theory

3. _____ was developed by Frederick Herzberg, a psychologist who found that job satisfaction and job dissatisfaction acted independently of each other. _____ states that there are certain factors in the workplace that cause job satisfaction, while a separate set of factors cause dissatisfaction.
   a. 1990 Clean Air Act
   b. Need for power
   c. Two-factor theory
   d. Need for Achievement

4. In organizational development (OD), _____ is the application of Socio-Technical Systems principles and techniques to the humanization of work.

   The aims of _____ to improved job satisfaction, to improved through-put, to improved quality and to reduced employee problems, e.g., grievances, absenteeism.

   Under scientific management people would be directed by reason and the problems of industrial unrest would be appropriately (i.e., scientifically) addressed.

Chapter 10. Motivation

a. Management process
b. Graduate recruitment
c. Path-goal theory
d. Work design

5. _____ is an attempt to motivate employees by giving them the opportunity to use the range of their abilities. It is an idea that was developed by the American psychologist Frederick Herzberg in the 1950s. It can be contrasted to job enlargement which simply increases the number of tasks without changing the challenge.

 a. Catfish effect
 b. C-A-K-E
 c. Cash cow
 d. Job enrichment

6. _____ attempts to explain relational satisfaction in terms of perceptions of fair/unfair distributions of resources within interpersonal relationships. _____ is considered as one of the justice theories, It was first developed in 1962 by John Stacey Adams, a workplace and behavioral psychologist, who asserted that employees seek to maintain equity between the inputs that they bring to a job and the outcomes that they receive from it against the perceived inputs and outcomes of others (Adams, 1965.) The belief is that people value fair treatment which causes them to be motivated to keep the fairness maintained within the relationships of their co-workers and the organization.

 a. A4e
 b. AAAI
 c. Equity theory
 d. A Stake in the Outcome

7. _____ is about the mental processes regarding choice, or choosing. It explains the processes that an individual undergoes to make choices. In organizational behavior study, _____ is a motivation theory first proposed by Victor Vroom of the Yale School of Management.

 a. A4e
 b. Expectancy theory
 c. AAAI
 d. A Stake in the Outcome

8. In business and accounting, _____s are everything of value that is owned by a person or company. Any property or object of value that one possesses, usually considered as applicable to the payment of one's debts is considered an _____. Simplistically stated, _____s are things of value that can be readily converted into cash.

a. AAAI
b. A Stake in the Outcome
c. Asset
d. A4e

9. _____ is the belief that one is capable of performing in a certain manner to attain certain goals. It is a belief that one has the capabilities to execute the courses of actions required to manage prospective situations. Unlike efficacy, which is the power to produce an effect (in essence, competence), _____ is the belief (whether or not accurate) that one has the power to produce that effect.
   a. 28-hour day
   b. 33 Strategies of War
   c. 1990 Clean Air Act
   d. Self-efficacy

10. _____ has become one of the most popular theories in organizational psychology.

Goal setting has been a formula used for acheivement since the early 1800s. The form and pattern has cahanged drastically over the years and there is still much debate as to what is the most efective pattern to follow.

   a. Human relations
   b. Job satisfaction
   c. Corporate Culture
   d. Goal-setting theory

11. In operant conditioning, _____ occurs when an event following a response causes an increase in the probability of that response occurring in the future. Response strength can be assessed by measures such as the frequency with which the response is made (for example, a pigeon may peck a key more times in the session), or the speed with which it is made (for example, a rat may run a maze faster.) The environment change contingent upon the response is called a reinforcer.
   a. Meetings, Incentives, Conferences, and Exhibitions
   b. Historiometry
   c. Diminishing Manufacturing Sources and Material Shortages
   d. Reinforcement

12. The _____, sometimes called the Puritan Work Ethic, is a sociological, theoretical concept. It is based upon the notion that the Calvinist emphasis on the necessity for hard work is proponent of a person's calling and worldly success is a sign of personal salvation. It is argued that Protestants beginning with Martin Luther had reconceptualised worldly work as a duty which benefits both the individual and society as a whole.

a. 33 Strategies of War
b. 28-hour day
c. Protestant work ethic
d. 1990 Clean Air Act

13. Within graph theory and network analysis, there are various measures of the _____ of a vertex within a graph that determine the relative importance of a vertex within the graph (for example, how important a person is within a social network, or, in the theory of space syntax, how important a room is within a building or how well-used a road is within an urban network.)

There are four measures of _____ that are widely used in network analysis: degree _____, betweenness, closeness, and eigenvector _____.

The first, and simplest, is degree _____.

a. 1990 Clean Air Act
b. 33 Strategies of War
c. 28-hour day
d. Centrality

14. _____ is a set of values based on hard work and diligence. It is also a belief in the moral benefit of work and its ability to enhance character. An example would be the Protestant _____.
a. 28-hour day
b. Work ethic
c. 33 Strategies of War
d. 1990 Clean Air Act

Chapter 11. Groups and Teams

1. _____ is one of the managerial functions like planning, organizing, staffing and directing. It is an important function because it helps to check the errors and to take the corrective action so that deviation from standards are minimized and stated goals of the organization are achieved in desired manner. According to modern concepts, _____ is a foreseeing action whereas earlier concept of _____ was used only when errors were detected. _____ in management means setting standards, measuring actual performance and taking corrective action.
   a. Control
   b. Turnover
   c. Schedule of reinforcement
   d. Decision tree pruning

2. In mathematics, a _____ law is (roughly speaking) a formal power series behaving as if it were the product of a Lie group. They were first defined in 1946 by S. Bochner. The term _____ sometimes means the same as _____ law, and sometimes means one of several generalizations.
   a. 33 Strategies of War
   b. 28-hour day
   c. 1990 Clean Air Act
   d. Formal group

3. The goal of most research on _____ is to learn why and how small groups change over time. To do this, researchers examine patterns of change and continuity in groups over time. Aspects of a group that might be studied include the quality of the output produced by a group, the type and frequency of its activities, its cohesiveness, the existence of conflict, etc.
   a. 1990 Clean Air Act
   b. 28-hour day
   c. 33 Strategies of War
   d. Group development

4. The 'business case for _____', theorizes that in a global marketplace, a company that employs a diverse workforce (both men and women, people of many generations, people from ethnically and racially diverse backgrounds etc.) is better able to understand the demographics of the marketplace it serves and is thus better equipped to thrive in that marketplace than a company that has a more limited range of employee demographics.

   An additional corollary suggests that a company that supports the _____ of its workforce can also improve employee satisfaction, productivity and retention.

   a. Virtual team
   b. Kanban
   c. Trademark
   d. Diversity

Chapter 11. Groups and Teams

5. In the social psychology of groups, _____ is the phenomenon of people making less effort to achieve a goal when they work in a group than when they work alone. This is seen as one of the main reasons groups are sometimes less productive than the combined performance of their members working as individuals.

- Ringelmann, Max : 1913

Research began in 1913 with Max Ringelmann's study. He found that when he asked a group of men to pull on a rope, that they did not pull as hard, or put as much effort into the activity, as they did when they were pulling alone.

   a. Personal space
   b. Self-enhancement
   c. Machiavellianism
   d. Social loafing

6. In economics, business, retail, and accounting, a _____ is the value of money that has been used up to produce something, and hence is not available for use anymore. In economics, a _____ is an alternative that is given up as a result of a decision. In business, the _____ may be one of acquisition, in which case the amount of money expended to acquire it is counted as _____.
   a. Fixed costs
   b. Cost overrun
   c. Cost allocation
   d. Cost

7. A _____ is a relatively new executive level position at a corporation, company, organization typically reporting directly to the CEO or board of directors. The _____ is responsible for a brand's image, experience, and promise, and propagating it throughout all aspects of the company. The brand officer oversees marketing, advertising, design, public relations and customer service departments.
   a. Chief executive officer
   b. Chief brand officer
   c. Director of communications
   d. Purchasing manager

8. _____ has been described as the 'process of social influence in which one person can enlist the aid and support of others in the accomplishment of a common task' . A definition more inclusive of followers comes from Alan Keith of Genentech who said '_____ is ultimately about creating a way for people to contribute to making something extraordinary happen.'

_____ is one of the most salient aspects of the organizational context. However, defining _____ has been challenging.

a. 1990 Clean Air Act
b. 28-hour day
c. Situational leadership
d. Leadership

9. '_____ is a conflict among the roles corresponding to two or more statuses.'

_____ is a special form of social conflict that takes place when one is forced to take on two different and incompatible roles at the same time. Consider the example of a doctor who is himself a patient, or who must decide whether he should be present for his daughter's birthday party (in his role as 'father') or attend an ailing patient (as 'doctor'.) (Also compare the psychological concept of cognitive dissonance.)

a. Role conflict
b. Soft skill
c. Self-disclosure
d. Social network analysis

10. Procter is a surname, and may also refer to:

- Bryan Waller Procter (pseud. Barry Cornwall), English poet
- Goodwin Procter, American law firm
- _____, consumer products multinational

a. Strict liability
b. Master and Servant Acts
c. Downstream
d. Procter ' Gamble

11. A _____ is a group of employees from various functional areas of the organization - research, engineering, marketing, finance. human resources, and operations, for example - who are all focused on a specific objective and are responsible to work as a team to improve coordination and innovation across divisions and resolve mutual problems.
a. Graduate recruitment
b. Cross-functional Team
c. Sociotechnical systems
d. Goal-setting theory

12. A _____ -- also known as a geographically dispersed team -- is a group of individuals who work across time, space, and organizational boundaries with links strengthened by webs of communication technology. They have complementary skills and are committed to a common purpose, have interdependent performance goals, and share an approach to work for which they hold themselves mutually accountable. Geographically dispersed teams allow organizations to hire and retain the best people regardless of location.
   a. Risk management
   b. Kanban
   c. Trademark
   d. Virtual Team

Chapter 12. Communication and Negotiation

1. _____ is an organization's process of defining its strategy and making decisions on allocating its resources to pursue this strategy, including its capital and people. Various business analysis techniques can be used in _____, including SWOT analysis (Strengths, Weaknesses, Opportunities, and Threats) and PEST analysis (Political, Economic, Social, and Technological analysis) or STEER analysis involving Socio-cultural, Technological, Economic, Ecological, and Regulatory factors and EPISTEL (Environment, Political, Informatic, Social, Technological, Economic and Legal)

_____ is the formal consideration of an organization's future course. All _____ deals with at least one of three key questions:

   1. 'What do we do?'
   2. 'For whom do we do it?'
   3. 'How do we excel?'

In business _____, the third question is better phrased 'How can we beat or avoid competition?'. (Bradford and Duncan, page 1.)

   a. 1990 Clean Air Act
   b. 33 Strategies of War
   c. Strategic planning
   d. 28-hour day

2. _____ is an advertisement in which a particular product specifically mentions a competitor by name for the express purpose of showing why the competitor is inferior to the product naming it.

This should not be confused with parody advertisements, where a fictional product is being advertised for the purpose of poking fun at the particular advertisement, nor should it be confused with the use of a coined brand name for the purpose of comparing the product without actually naming an actual competitor. ('Wikipedia tastes better and is less filling than the Encyclopedia Galactica.')

In the 1980s, during what has been referred to as the cola wars, soft-drink manufacturer Pepsi ran a series of advertisements where people, caught on hidden camera, in a blind taste test, chose Pepsi over rival Coca-Cola.

   a. 33 Strategies of War
   b. Comparative advertising
   c. 1990 Clean Air Act
   d. 28-hour day

3. A _____ is defined as someone who controls access to something. It also refers to individuals who decide whether a given message will be distributed by a mass medium.

_____s serve several different purposes such as academic admissions, financial advising, and news editing.

Chapter 12. Communication and Negotiation

a. 33 Strategies of War
b. 1990 Clean Air Act
c. Gatekeeper
d. 28-hour day

4. _____ is a recursive process where two or more people or organizations work together in an intersection of common goals -- for example, an intellectual endeavor that is creative in nature--by sharing knowledge, learning and building consensus. _____ does not require leadership and can sometimes bring better results through decentralization and egalitarianism. In particular, teams that work collaboratively can obtain greater resources, recognition and reward when facing competition for finite resources._____ is also present in opposing goals exhibiting the notion of adversarial _____, though this is not a common case for using the term.

   a. 28-hour day
   b. 1990 Clean Air Act
   c. Collectivism
   d. Collaboration

5. Procter is a surname, and may also refer to:

   - Bryan Waller Procter (pseud. Barry Cornwall), English poet
   - Goodwin Procter, American law firm
   - _____, consumer products multinational

   a. Downstream
   b. Strict liability
   c. Master and Servant Acts
   d. Procter ' Gamble

Chapter 13. Operations Management

1. _____ is an area of business concerned with the production of goods and services, and involves the responsibility of ensuring that business operations are efficient in terms of using as little resource as needed, and effective in terms of meeting customer requirements. It is concerned with managing the process that converts inputs (in the forms of materials, labour and energy) into outputs (in the form of goods and services.)

Operations traditionally refers to the production of goods and services separately, although the distinction between these two main types of operations is increasingly difficult to make as manufacturers tend to merge product and service offerings.

   a. AAAI
   b. Operations management
   c. A Stake in the Outcome
   d. A4e

2. In economics, business, retail, and accounting, a _____ is the value of money that has been used up to produce something, and hence is not available for use anymore. In economics, a _____ is an alternative that is given up as a result of a decision. In business, the _____ may be one of acquisition, in which case the amount of money expended to acquire it is counted as _____.
   a. Cost overrun
   b. Cost allocation
   c. Cost
   d. Fixed costs

3. _____ is one of the managerial functions like planning, organizing, staffing and directing. It is an important function because it helps to check the errors and to take the corrective action so that deviation from standards are minimized and stated goals of the organization are achieved in desired manner. According to modern concepts, _____ is a foreseeing action whereas earlier concept of _____ was used only when errors were detected. _____ in management means setting standards, measuring actual performance and taking corrective action.
   a. Schedule of reinforcement
   b. Decision tree pruning
   c. Turnover
   d. Control

4. The _____ in statistical process control is a tool used to determine whether a manufacturing or business process is in a state of statistical control or not.

If the chart indicates that the process is currently under control then it can be used with confidence to predict the future performance of the process. If the chart indicates that the process being monitored is not in control, the pattern it reveals can help determine the source of variation to be eliminated to bring the process back into control.

a. Failure rate
b. Control chart
c. Time series analysis
d. Simple moving average

5. _____ is an effective method of monitoring a process through the use of control charts. Control charts enable the use of objective criteria for distinguishing background variation from events of significance based on statistical techniques. Much of its power lies in the ability to monitor both process center and its variation about that center.

a. Quality control
b. Statistical process control
c. Single Minute Exchange of Die
d. Process capability

6. _____ is a business management strategy aimed at embedding awareness of quality in all organizational processes. _____ has been widely used in manufacturing, education, hospitals, call centers, government, and service industries, as well as NASA space and science programs.

As defined by the International Organization for Standardization (ISO):

'_____ is a management approach for an organization, centered on quality, based on the participation of all its members and aiming at long-term success through customer satisfaction, and benefits to all members of the organization and to society.' ISO 8402:1994

One major aim is to reduce variation from every process so that greater consistency of effort is obtained. (Royse, D., Thyer, B., Padgett D., ' Logan T., 2006)

a. 1990 Clean Air Act
b. 28-hour day
c. Quality management
d. Total quality management

7. _____ can be considered to have three main components: quality control, quality assurance and quality improvement. _____ is focused not only on product quality, but also the means to achieve it. _____ therefore uses quality assurance and control of processes as well as products to achieve more consistent quality.

a. 1990 Clean Air Act
b. Total quality management
c. 28-hour day
d. Quality management

Chapter 13. Operations Management

8. A _____ or business method is a collection of related, structured activities or tasks that produce a specific service or product (serve a particular goal) for a particular customer or customers. It often can be visualized with a flowchart as a sequence of activities.

There are three types of _____ es:

1. Management processes, the processes that govern the operation of a system. Typical management processes include 'Corporate Governance' and 'Strategic Management'.
2. Operational processes, processes that constitute the core business and create the primary value stream. Typical operational processes are Purchasing, Manufacturing, Marketing, and Sales.
3. Supporting processes, which support the core processes. Examples include Accounting, Recruitment, Technical support.

A _____ begins with a customer's need and ends with a customer's need fulfillment. Process oriented organizations break down the barriers of structural departments and try to avoid functional silos.

a. 28-hour day
b. 1990 Clean Air Act
c. 33 Strategies of War
d. Business process

9. In probability theory, a probability distribution is called _____ if its cumulative distribution function is _____. This is equivalent to saying that for random variables X with the distribution in question, Pr[X = a] = 0 for all real numbers a, i.e.: the probability that X attains the value a is zero, for any number a. If the distribution of X is _____ then X is called a _____ random variable.

a. Connectionist expert systems
b. Decision tree pruning
c. Continuous
d. Pay Band

10. _____ is an inventory strategy that strives to improve the return on investment of a business by reducing in-process inventory and its associated carrying costs. To meet _____ objectives, the process relies on signals between different points in the process. This means the process is often driven by a series of signals, or Kanban , which tell production when to make the next part. Kanban are usually 'tickets' but can be simple visual signals, such as the presence or absence of a part on a shelf. Implemented correctly, _____ can dramatically improve a manufacturing organization's return on investment, quality, and efficiency.

a. 1990 Clean Air Act
b. 33 Strategies of War
c. 28-hour day
d. Just-in-time

Chapter 13. Operations Management

11. The _____ is given by the United States National Institute of Standards and Technology. Through the actions of the National Productivity Advisory Committee chaired by Jack Grayson, it was established by the Malcolm Baldrige National Quality Improvement Act of 1987 - Public Law 100-107 and named for Malcolm Baldrige, who served as United States Secretary of Commerce during the Reagan administration from 1981 until his 1987 death in a rodeo accident. APQC, , organized the first White House Conference on Productivity, spearheading the creation and design of the _____ in 1987, and jointly administering the award for its first three years.
    a. Business Network Transformation
    b. Scenario planning
    c. Time and attendance
    d. Malcolm Baldrige National Quality Award

12. _____ is a Japanese philosophy that focuses on continuous improvement throughout all aspects of life. When applied to the workplace, _____ activities continually improve all functions of a business, from manufacturing to management and from the CEO to the assembly line workers. By improving standardized activities and processes, _____ aims to eliminate waste .
    a. Sensitivity analysis
    b. Psychological pricing
    c. Cross-docking
    d. Kaizen

13. In organizational development (OD), _____ is a series of actions taken by a Process Owner to identify, analyze and improve existing processes within an organization to meet new goals and objectives. These actions often follow a specific methodology or strategy to create successful results. A sampling of these are listed below.
    a. Product innovation
    b. Process improvement
    c. Supervisory board
    d. Letter of resignation

14. _____ refers to increasing the spiritual, political, social or economic strength of individuals and communities. It often involves the empowered developing confidence in their own capacities.

The term Human _____ covers a vast landscape of meanings, interpretations, definitions and disciplines ranging from psychology and philosophy to the highly commercialized Self-Help industry and Motivational sciences.

Chapter 13. Operations Management

a. AAAI
b. Empowerment
c. A Stake in the Outcome
d. A4e

15. _____ is a business management strategy, initially implemented by Motorola, that today enjoys widespread application in many sectors of industry.

_____ seeks to improve the quality of process outputs by identifying and removing the causes of defects (errors) and variation in manufacturing and business processes. It uses a set of quality management methods, including statistical methods, and creates a special infrastructure of people within the organization ('Black Belts' etc.)

a. Takt time
b. Production line
c. Theory of constraints
d. Six Sigma

16. _____ is the process of determining the production capacity needed by an organization to meet changing demands for its products. In the context of _____, 'capacity' is the maximum amount of work that an organization is capable of completing in a given period of time.

A discrepancy between the capacity of an organization and the demands of its customers results in inefficiency, either in under-utilized resources or unfulfilled customers.

a. Scientific management
b. Productivity
c. Remanufacturing
d. Capacity planning

17. _____ is a business term used to define an inventory categorization technique often used in materials management.

_____ provides a mechanism for identifying items which will have a significant impact on overall inventory cost whilst also providing a mechanism for identifying different categories of stock that will require different management and controls

When carrying out an _____, inventory items are valued (item cost multiplied by quantity issued/consumed in period) with the results then ranked. The results are then grouped typically into three bands.

Chapter 13. Operations Management

a. ABC analysis
b. A4e
c. A Stake in the Outcome
d. AAAI

18. _____ is the level of inventory that minimizes the total inventory holding costs and ordering costs. The framework used to determine this order quantity is also known as Wilson _____ Model. The model was developed by F. W. Harris in 1913.

a. Anti-leadership
b. Event management
c. Economic order quantity
d. Effective executive

19. The _____, is a mathematically based algorithm for scheduling a set of project activities. It is an important tool for effective project management.

It was developed in the 1950s by the Dupont Corporation at about the same time that General Dynamics and the US Navy were developing the Program Evaluation and Review Technique (PERT) Today, it is commonly used with all forms of projects, including construction, software development, research projects, product development, engineering, and plant maintenance, among others.

a. 33 Strategies of War
b. 1990 Clean Air Act
c. 28-hour day
d. Critical path method

20. A _____ is a type of bar chart that illustrates a project schedule. _____s illustrate the start and finish dates of the terminal elements and summary elements of a project. Terminal elements and summary elements comprise the work breakdown structure of the project.

a. 33 Strategies of War
b. Gantt chart
c. 1990 Clean Air Act
d. 28-hour day

21. _____ refers to metrics and measures of output from production processes, per unit of input. Labor _____, for example, is typically measured as a ratio of output per labor-hour, an input. _____ may be conceived of as a metrics of the technical or engineering efficiency of production.

Chapter 13. Operations Management

a. Master production schedule
b. Remanufacturing
c. Value engineering
d. Productivity

22. _____ is the amount of goods and services that a labourer produces in a given amount of time. It is one of several types of productivity that economists measure. _____ can be measured for a firm, a process or a country.

a. Time and attendance
b. Labour productivity
c. Retroactive overtime
d. Business Network Transformation

23. In business and accounting, _____s are everything of value that is owned by a person or company. Any property or object of value that one possesses, usually considered as applicable to the payment of one's debts is considered an _____. Simplistically stated, _____s are things of value that can be readily converted into cash.

a. A4e
b. AAAI
c. A Stake in the Outcome
d. Asset

24. _____, in microeconomics, are the cost advantages that a business obtains due to expansion. They are factors that cause a producer's average cost per unit to fall as scale is increased. _____ is a long run concept and refers to reductions in unit cost as the size of a facility, or scale, increases.

a. A Stake in the Outcome
b. A4e
c. Economies of scope
d. Economies of scale

25. A _____ is a business efficiency technique combining the Time Study work of Frederick Winslow Taylor with the Motion Study work of Frank and Lillian Gilbreth (not to be confused with their son, best known through the biographical 1950 film and book Cheaper by the Dozen.) It is a major part of scientific management (Taylorism.)

A _____ would be used to reduce the number of motions in performing a task in order to increase productivity.

Chapter 13. Operations Management

a. Prevailing wage
b. Total benefits of ownership
c. Time and motion study
d. Manufacturing operations

26. An _____ is a manufacturing process in which parts (usually interchangeable parts) are added to a product in a sequential manner using optimally planned logistics to create a finished product much faster than with handcrafting-type methods. The _____ developed by Ford Motor Company between 1908 and 1915 made _____s famous in the following decade through the social ramifications of mass production, such as the affordability of the Ford Model T and the introduction of high wages for Ford workers. However, the various preconditions for the development at Ford stretched far back into the 19th century, from the gradual realization of the dream of interchangeability, to the concept of reinventing workflow and job descriptions using analytical methods.

   a. A4e
   b. Assembly line
   c. A Stake in the Outcome
   d. AAAI

27. _____ are typically small manufacturing operations that handle specialized manufacturing processes such as small customer orders or small batch jobs. _____ typically move on to different jobs (possibly with different customers) when each job is completed. By nature of this type of manufacturing operation, _____ are usually specialized in skill and processes.

   a. 28-hour day
   b. 1990 Clean Air Act
   c. Job shops
   d. 33 Strategies of War

28. _____ is the production of large amounts of standardized products, including and especially on assembly lines. The concepts of _____ are applied to various kinds of products, from fluids and particulates handled in bulk to discrete solid parts to assemblies of such parts

   _____ of assemblies typically uses electric-motor-powered moving tracks or conveyor belts to move partially complete products to workers, who perform simple repetitive tasks.

   a. 28-hour day
   b. Mass production
   c. 1990 Clean Air Act
   d. 33 Strategies of War

Chapter 13. Operations Management

29. _____ is the use of information technology to support engineers in tasks such as analysis, simulation, design, manufacture, planning, diagnosis, and repair.

Software tools that have been developed to support these activities are considered CAE tools. CAE tools are being used, for example, to analyze the robustness and performance of components and assemblies.

a. 1990 Clean Air Act
b. Computer-aided engineering
c. 33 Strategies of War
d. 28-hour day

30. _____ is the use of computer-based software tools that assist engineers and machinists in manufacturing or prototyping product components. Its primary purpose is to create a faster production process and components with more precise dimensions and material consistency, which in some cases, uses only the required amount of raw material (thus minimizing waste), while simultaneously reducing energy consumption. CAM is a programming tool that makes it possible to manufacture physical models using computer-aided design (CAD) programs.
a. Computer-aided manufacturing
b. 28-hour day
c. 33 Strategies of War
d. 1990 Clean Air Act

31. A _____ system is a manufacturing system in which there is some amount of flexibility that allows the system to react in the case of changes, whether predicted or unpredicted. This flexibility is generally considered to fall into two categories, which both contain numerous subcategories.

The first category, machine flexibility, covers the system's ability to be changed to produce new product types, and ability to change the order of operations executed on a part. The second category is called routing flexibility, which consists of the ability to use multiple machines to perform the same operation on a part, as well as the system's ability to absorb large-scale changes, such as in volume, capacity, or capability.

a. Homeworkers
b. Manufacturing resource planning
c. Jidoka
d. Flexible manufacturing

32. A _____ is the system of organizations, people, technology, activities, information and resources involved in moving a product or service from supplier to customer. _____ activities transform natural resources, raw materials and components into a finished product that is delivered to the end customer. In sophisticated _____ systems, used products may re-enter the _____ at any point where residual value is recyclable.

a. Supply chain
b. Drop shipping
c. Packaging
d. Wholesalers

Chapter 14. Control

1. _____ is one of the managerial functions like planning, organizing, staffing and directing. It is an important function because it helps to check the errors and to take the corrective action so that deviation from standards are minimized and stated goals of the organization are achieved in desired manner. According to modern concepts, _____ is a foreseeing action whereas earlier concept of _____ was used only when errors were detected. _____ in management means setting standards, measuring actual performance and taking corrective action.
   a. Turnover
   b. Schedule of reinforcement
   c. Decision tree pruning
   d. Control

2. _____ describes the situation when output from (or information about the result of) an event or phenomenon in the past will influence the same event/phenomenon in the present or future. When an event is part of a chain of cause-and-effect that forms a circuit or loop, then the event is said to 'feed back' into itself.

   _____ is also a synonym for:

   - _____ signal; the information about the initial event that is the basis for subsequent modification of the event.
   - _____ loop; the causal path that leads from the initial generation of the _____ signal to the subsequent modification of the event.

   _____ is a mechanism, process or signal that is looped back to control a system within itself. Such a loop is called a _____ loop.

   a. Feedback loop
   b. Feedback
   c. Positive feedback
   d. 1990 Clean Air Act

3. Feedback describes the situation when output from (or information about the result of) an event or phenomenon in the past will influence the same event/phenomenon in the present or future. When an event is part of a chain of cause-and-effect that forms a circuit or loop, then the event is said to 'feed back' into itself.

   Feedback is also a synonym for:

   - Feedback signal; the information about the initial event that is the basis for subsequent modification of the event.
   - _____; the causal path that leads from the initial generation of the feedback signal to the subsequent modification of the event.

   Feedback is a mechanism, process or signal that is looped back to control a system within itself. Such a loop is called a _____.

a. 1990 Clean Air Act
b. Positive feedback
c. Negative feedback
d. Feedback loop

4. _____ is the process by which the activities of an organisation, particularly those regarding decision-making, become concentrated within a particular location and/or group.

a. Product innovation
b. Chief operating officer
c. Corner office
d. Centralization

5. _____ is a term that refers both to:

- a formal discipline used to help appraise, or assess, the case for a project or proposal, which itself is a process known as project appraisal; and
- an informal approach to making decisions of any kind.

Under both definitions the process involves, whether explicitly or implicitly, weighing the total expected costs against the total expected benefits of one or more actions in order to choose the best or most profitable option. The formal process is often referred to as either CBA (_____) or BCost-benefit analysis

A hallmark of CBA is that all benefits and all costs are expressed in money terms, and are adjusted for the time value of money, so that all flows of benefits and flows of project costs over time (which tend to occur at different points in time) are expressed on a common basis in terms of their 'present value.' Closely related, but slightly different, formal techniques include Cost-effectiveness analysis, Economic impact analysis, Fiscal impact analysis and Social Return on Investment(SROI) analysis. The latter builds upon the logic of _____, but differs in that it is explicitly designed to inform the practical decision-making of enterprise managers and investors focused on optimising their social and environmental impacts.

a. Cost-benefit analysis
b. Kepner-Tregoe
c. Gittins index
d. Decision engineering

6. In finance, a _____ or accounting ratio is a ratio of two selected numerical values taken from an enterprise's financial statements. There are many standard ratios used to try to evaluate the overall financial condition of a corporation or other organization. _____s may be used by managers within a firm, by current and potential shareholders (owners) of a firm, and by a firm's creditors.

a. Rate of return
b. Return on sales
c. Return on equity
d. Financial ratio

7. _____(requity)measures the rate of return on the ownership interest (shareholders' equity) of the common stock owners. It measures a firm's efficiency at generating profits from every dollar of shareholders' equity (also known as net assets or assets minus liabilities.) It shows how well a company uses investment dollars to generate earnings growth.
   a. Return on equity
   b. Return on Capital Employed
   c. Financial ratio
   d. Rate of return

8. In economics ' business, specifically cost accounting, the _____ is the point at which cost or expenses and revenue are equal: there is no net loss or gain, and one has 'broken even'. A profit or a loss has not been made, although opportunity costs have been paid, and capital has received the risk-adjusted, expected return.

   For example, if the business sells less than 200 tables each month, it will make a loss, if it sells more, it will be a profit.

   a. Fixed asset turnover
   b. Virtuous circle
   c. Defined benefit pension plan
   d. Break-even point

9. _____ are a set of documents that describe an organization's policies for operation and the procedures necessary to fulfill the policies. They are often initiated because of some external requirement, such as environmental compliance or other governmental regulations, such as the American Sarbanes-Oxley Act requiring full openness in accounting practices. The easiest way to start writing _____ is to interview the users of the _____ and create a flow chart or task map or work flow of the process from start to finish.
   a. Customer retention
   b. Horizontal integration
   c. Group booking
   d. Policies and procedures

10. _____ is an advertisement in which a particular product specifically mentions a competitor by name for the express purpose of showing why the competitor is inferior to the product naming it.

This should not be confused with parody advertisements, where a fictional product is being advertised for the purpose of poking fun at the particular advertisement, nor should it be confused with the use of a coined brand name for the purpose of comparing the product without actually naming an actual competitor. ('Wikipedia tastes better and is less filling than the Encyclopedia Galactica.')

In the 1980s, during what has been referred to as the cola wars, soft-drink manufacturer Pepsi ran a series of advertisements where people, caught on hidden camera, in a blind taste test, chose Pepsi over rival Coca-Cola.

   a. 1990 Clean Air Act
   b. 28-hour day
   c. Comparative advertising
   d. 33 Strategies of War

11. _____ is the use of an object (typically referred to as an RFID tag) applied to or incorporated into a product, animal, or person for the purpose of identification and tracking using radio waves. Some tags can be read from several meters away and beyond the line of sight of the reader.

Most RFID tags contain at least two parts.

   a. 1990 Clean Air Act
   b. 28-hour day
   c. 33 Strategies of War
   d. Radio-frequency identification

12. The _____ is a performance management tool for measuring whether the smaller-scale operational activities of a company are aligned with its larger-scale objectives in terms of vision and strategy.

By focusing not only on financial outcomes but also on the operational, marketing and developmental inputs to these, the _____ helps provide a more comprehensive view of a business, which in turn helps organizations act in their best long-term interests. This tool is also being used to address business response to climate change and greenhouse gas emissions.

   a. Commercial management
   b. Middle management
   c. Balanced scorecard
   d. Management development

Chapter 15. Organizational Change and Development

1. _____ is a structured approach to transitioning individuals, teams, and organizations from a current state to a desired future state. The current definition of _____ includes both organizational _____ processes and individual _____ models, which together are used to manage the people side of change.

A number of models are available for understanding the transitioning of individuals through the phases of _____ and strengthening organizational development initiative in both government and corporate sectors.

   a. Change management
   b. 28-hour day
   c. 33 Strategies of War
   d. 1990 Clean Air Act

2. _____ is an influential development in the field of social science. It provides a framework for looking at the factors (forces) that influence a situation, originally social situations. It looks at forces that are either driving movement toward a goal (helping forces) or blocking movement toward a goal (hindering forces.)
   a. Logistics management
   b. Board of governors
   c. Dynamic Enterprise Modeling
   d. Force field analysis

3. A _____ is an alliance among individuals or groups, during which they cooperate in joint action, each in his own self-interest, joining forces together for a common cause. This alliance may be temporary or a matter of convenience. A _____ thus differs from a more formal covenant.
   a. 1990 Clean Air Act
   b. 33 Strategies of War
   c. 28-hour day
   d. Coalition

4. In economics and sociology, an _____ is any factor (financial or non-financial) that enables or motivates a particular course of action, or counts as a reason for preferring one choice to the alternatives. It is an expectation that encourages people to behave in a certain way. Since human beings are purposeful creatures, the study of _____ structures is central to the study of all economic activity (both in terms of individual decision-making and in terms of co-operation and competition within a larger institutional structure.)
   a. AAAI
   b. A4e
   c. A Stake in the Outcome
   d. Incentive

Chapter 15. Organizational Change and Development

5. In game theory, an _____ is a set of moves or strategies taken by the players, or their payoffs resulting from the actions or strategies taken by all players. The two are complementary in that given knowledge of the set of strategies of all players, the final state of the game is known, as are any relevant payoffs. In a game where chance or a random event is involved, the _____ is not known from only the set of strategies, but is only realized when the random event(s) are realized.
    a. A Stake in the Outcome
    b. AAAI
    c. A4e
    d. Outcome

6. As defined by Richard Beckhard, _____ is a planned, top-down, organization-wide effort to increase the organization's effectiveness and health. _____ is achieved through interventions in the organization's 'processes,' using behavioural science knowledge. According to Warren Bennis, _____ is a complex strategy intended to change the beliefs, attitudes, values, and structure of organizations so that they can better adapt to new technologies, markets, and challenges.
    a. Organizational development
    b. Organizational structure
    c. Informal organization
    d. Organizational culture

7. _____ is the process of comparing the cost, cycle time, productivity, or quality of a specific process or method to another that is widely considered to be an industry standard or best practice. Essentially, _____ provides a snapshot of the performance of your business and helps you understand where you are in relation to a particular standard. The result is often a business case for making changes in order to make improvements.
    a. Competitive heterogeneity
    b. Complementors
    c. Benchmarking
    d. Cost leadership

8. A _____ is a form of qualitative research in which a group of people are asked about their attitude towards a product, service, concept, advertisement, idea, or packaging. Questions are asked in an interactive group setting where participants are free to talk with other group members.

The first _____s were created at the Bureau of Applied Social Research by associate director, sociologist Robert K. Merton.

Chapter 15. Organizational Change and Development

a. Marketing research
b. Market analysis
c. 1990 Clean Air Act
d. Focus group

9. A _____ is the term given to a company that facilitates the learning of its members and continuously transforms itself. _____s develop as a result of the pressures facing modern organizations and enables them to remain competitive in the business environment. A _____ has five main features; systems thinking, personal mastery, mental models, shared vision and team learning.

a. 1990 Clean Air Act
b. Quality function deployment
c. Learning organization
d. Hoshin Kanri

10. _____ is an area of knowledge within organizational theory that studies models and theories about the way an organization learns and adapts.

In Organizational development (OD), learning is a characteristic of an adaptive organization, i.e., an organization that is able to sense changes in signals from its environment (both internal and external) and adapt accordingly.

a. A Stake in the Outcome
b. AAAI
c. Organizational learning
d. A4e

11. The _____ was the outcome of the failure of negotiating governments to create the International Trade Organization (ITO.) GATT was formed in 1947 and lasted until 1994, when it was replaced by the World Trade Organization. The Bretton Woods Conference had introduced the idea for an organization to regulate trade as part of a larger plan for economic recovery after World War II.

a. Multilateral treaty
b. General Agreement on Tariffs and Trade
c. 1990 Clean Air Act
d. 28-hour day

12. The _____ was a period in the late 18th and early 19th centuries when major changes in agriculture, manufacturing, mining, and transportation had a profound effect on the socioeconomic and cultural conditions in Britain. The changes subsequently spread throughout Europe, North America, and eventually the world. The onset of the _____ marked a major turning point in human society; almost every aspect of daily life was eventually influenced in some way.

a. Abraham Harold Maslow
b. Industrial Revolution
c. Affiliation
d. Adam Smith

13. _____ is a theory of management that analyzes and synthesizes workflows, with the objective of improving labour productivity. The core ideas of the theory were developed by Frederick Winslow Taylor in the 1880s and 1890s, and were first published in his monographs, Shop Management and The Principles of _____ Taylor believed that decisions based upon tradition and rules of thumb should be replaced by precise procedures developed after careful study of an individual at work.

a. Scientific management
b. Master production schedule
c. Value engineering
d. Capacity planning

14. A _____ is a list of the general tasks and responsibilities of a position. Typically, it also includes to whom the position reports, specifications such as the qualifications needed by the person in the job, salary range for the position, etc. A _____ is usually developed by conducting a job analysis, which includes examining the tasks and sequences of tasks necessary to perform the job.

a. Job description
b. Recruitment
c. Recruitment advertising
d. Recruitment Process Insourcing

15. The sociologist Max Weber defined _____ as 'resting on devotion to the exceptional sanctity, heroism or exemplary character of an individual person, and of the normative patterns or order revealed or ordained by him.' _____ is one of three forms of authority laid out in Weber's tripartite classification of authority, the other two being traditional authority and rational-legal authority. The concept has acquired wide usage among sociologists.

In his writings about _____, Weber applies the term charisma to 'a certain quality of an individual personality, by virtue of which he is set apart from ordinary men and treated as endowed with supernatural, superhuman, or at least specifically exceptional powers or qualities.

a. 1990 Clean Air Act
b. Rational-legal authority
c. 28-hour day
d. Charismatic authority

16. _____ is a form of leadership in which the authority of an organization or a ruling regime is largely tied to tradition or custom. The main reason for the given state of affairs is that it 'has always been that way'.

In sociology, the concept of _____ comes from Max Weber's tripartite classification of authority, the other two forms being charismatic authority and rational-legal authority.

   a. 1990 Clean Air Act
   b. 28-hour day
   c. Rational-legal authority
   d. Traditional authority

17. _____ is a form of leadership in which the authority of an organization or a ruling regime is largely tied to legal rationality, legal legitimacy and bureaucracy. The majority of the modern states of the twentieth century are rational-legal authorities, according to those who use this form of classification.

In sociology, the concept of rational-legal domination comes from Max Weber's tripartite classification of authority; the other two forms being traditional authority and charismatic authority.

   a. Traditional authority
   b. 28-hour day
   c. Rational-legal authority
   d. 1990 Clean Air Act

18. The _____ is a form of reactivity whereby subjects improve an aspect of their behavior being experimentally measured simply in response to the fact that they are being studied, not in response to any particular experimental manipulation.

The term was coined in 1955 by Henry A. Landsberger when analyzing older experiments from 1924-1932 at the Hawthorne Works (outside Chicago.) Hawthorne Works had commissioned a study to see if its workers would become more productive in higher or lower levels of light.

   a. 28-hour day
   b. 1990 Clean Air Act
   c. 33 Strategies of War
   d. Hawthorne effect

19. _____ Movement refers to those researchers of organizational development who study the behavior of people in groups, in particular workplace groups. It originated in the 1920s' Hawthorne studies, which examined the effects of social relations, motivation and employee satisfaction on factory productivity. The movement viewed workers in terms of their psychology and fit with companies, rather than as interchangeable parts.

Chapter 15. Organizational Change and Development

a. Work design
b. Human relations
c. Participatory management
d. Hersey-Blanchard situational theory

20. _____ is an increasingly broadening term with which an organization, or other human system describes the combination of traditionally administrative personnel functions with acquisition and application of skills, knowledge and experience, Employee Relations and resource planning at various levels. The field draws upon concepts developed in Industrial/Organizational Psychology and System Theory. _____ has at least two related interpretations depending on context. The original usage derives from political economy and economics, where it was traditionally called labor, one of four factors of production although this perspective is changing as a function of new and ongoing research into more strategic approaches at national levels. This first usage is used more in terms of '_____ development', and can go beyond just organizations to the level of nations. The more traditional usage within corporations and businesses refers to the individuals within a firm or agency, and to the portion of the organization that deals with hiring, firing, training, and other personnel issues, typically referred to as `_____ management'.
    a. Human resources
    b. Progressive discipline
    c. Human resource management
    d. Bradford Factor

21. _____ is a concept based on the fact that rationality of individuals is limited by the information they have, the cognitive limitations of their minds, and the finite amount of time they have to make decisions. This contrasts with the concept of rationality as optimization. Another way to look at _____ is that, because decision-makers lack the ability and resources to arrive at the optimal solution, they instead apply their rationality only after having greatly simplified the choices available.
    a. Complete information
    b. Transferable utility
    c. Mixed strategy
    d. Bounded rationality

22. _____, is the discipline of using scientific research-based principles, strategies, and other analytical methods, such as mathematical modeling to improve any organization's ability to enact rational, meaningful business management decisions.
    a. Cross ownership
    b. Workflow
    c. Trustee
    d. Management science

Chapter 15. Organizational Change and Development

23. _____ in the USA, Canada, South Africa and Australia, and operational research in Europe, is an interdisciplinary branch of applied mathematics and formal science that uses methods such as mathematical modeling, statistics, and algorithms to arrive at optimal or near optimal solutions to complex problems. It is typically concerned with optimizing the maxima (profit, assembly line performance, crop yield, bandwidth, etc) or minima (loss, risk, etc.) of some objective function.
   a. AAAI
   b. A Stake in the Outcome
   c. Operations research
   d. A4e

24. _____ can be regarded as an outcome of mental processes (cognitive process) leading to the selection of a course of action among several alternatives. Every _____ process produces a final choice. The output can be an action or an opinion of choice.
   a. 33 Strategies of War
   b. 1990 Clean Air Act
   c. 28-hour day
   d. Decision making

25. _____ is an interdisciplinary field of science and the study of the nature of complex systems in nature, society, and science. More specifically, it is a framework by which one can analyze and/or describe any group of objects that work in concert to produce some result. This could be a single organism, any organization or society, or any electro-mechanical or informational artifact.
   a. 28-hour day
   b. 1990 Clean Air Act
   c. Systems Theory
   d. Systems thinking

ANSWER KEY

Chapter 1
1. a 2. d 3. d 4. d 5. d 6. d 7. c 8. d 9. a 10. b
11. d 12. d 13. d 14. a 15. d 16. b 17. d 18. a 19. d 20. d

Chapter 2
1. d 2. c 3. b 4. a 5. a 6. d 7. a 8. d 9. d

Chapter 3
1. a 2. b 3. a 4. d 5. d 6. c 7. d 8. a 9. b 10. d
11. b 12. d 13. d 14. d 15. c 16. d

Chapter 4
1. b 2. d 3. c 4. b 5. b 6. b 7. a 8. a 9. d 10. c
11. a 12. d 13. d 14. d 15. b 16. d

Chapter 5
1. d 2. d 3. a 4. d 5. d 6. d 7. b 8. b 9. b 10. c
11. c 12. d 13. d 14. d 15. c 16. b 17. a 18. b 19. c 20. b
21. a 22. d

Chapter 6
1. d 2. a 3. b 4. b 5. b 6. d 7. a 8. d 9. d 10. d
11. b 12. c 13. a

Chapter 7
1. b 2. c 3. c 4. b 5. d 6. d 7. d 8. d 9. a 10. d
11. d 12. d 13. d 14. a 15. d

Chapter 8
1. a 2. c 3. c 4. d 5. b 6. d 7. c 8. d 9. d 10. d
11. b 12. a 13. d 14. b 15. d 16. d 17. c 18. b 19. d 20. d
21. a 22. a 23. d 24. d 25. d 26. d 27. d 28. d 29. c 30. d
31. d 32. d 33. a 34. d 35. b 36. d 37. d 38. b 39. d 40. d
41. c 42. d 43. a 44. d 45. d

Chapter 9
1. d 2. d 3. d 4. d 5. d 6. c 7. d 8. c 9. d 10. a
11. d 12. c

Chapter 10
1. b 2. d 3. c 4. d 5. d 6. c 7. b 8. c 9. d 10. d
11. d 12. c 13. d 14. b

Chapter 11
1. a 2. d 3. d 4. d 5. d 6. d 7. b 8. d 9. a 10. d
11. b 12. d

Chapter 12
1. c   2. b   3. c   4. d   5. d

Chapter 13
1. b   2. c   3. d   4. b   5. b   6. d   7. d   8. d   9. c   10. d
11. d   12. d   13. b   14. b   15. d   16. d   17. a   18. c   19. d   20. b
21. d   22. b   23. d   24. d   25. c   26. b   27. c   28. b   29. b   30. a
31. d   32. a

Chapter 14
1. d   2. b   3. d   4. d   5. a   6. d   7. a   8. d   9. d   10. c
11. d   12. c

Chapter 15
1. a   2. d   3. d   4. d   5. d   6. a   7. c   8. d   9. c   10. c
11. b   12. b   13. a   14. a   15. d   16. d   17. c   18. d   19. b   20. a
21. d   22. d   23. c   24. d   25. c

www.ingramcontent.com/pod-product-compliance
Lightning Source LLC
Chambersburg PA
CBHW081848230426
43669CB00018B/2866